D0249507

FAMOUS CRIMES

Stories of Law and Order in Minnesota

By Sheri O'Meara and Merle Minda

the *Minnesota* series

150 YEARS
of STATEHOOD
1858·2008

Welcome to *Famous Crimes*

I n *Famous Crimes*, the fifth book in The Minnesota Series, you'll find stories and rare photographs about major criminal events in Minnesota. Inside, look back on and learn about major Minnesota cases of law and order and their surrounding events. Previous books in the series include *Storms!*, *Music Legends*, *Media Tales* and *Storms 2*. Pick up books at retailers across the state or order online at www.minnesotaseries.com.

Authors **Merle Minda, Sheri O'Meara**
Design and Layout **Phil Tippin**
Proofreader **Marsha Kitchel**
Web Consultant **Risdall Advertising, New Brighton, Minn.**
Printing **Bang Printing, Brainerd, Minn.**
Photographs **D Media Services**
Publishers **D Media: Debra Gustafson Decker, Dale Decker**

ISBN 9780978795658

Library of Congress Control Number: 2008922088

Cover photos: Associated Press, UMD, Minnesota Historical Society,
Interior photos: D Media Services, File Photos

Contents

Foreword

I remember the day we were gathered around the TV monitors in the newsroom ... watching a crime scene unfold in Miami. Someone had just shot fashion designer Gianni Versace. Within the hour—many of us still glued to our sets—Bernie Grace was on the phone from his car. The longtime KARE-TV crime reporter had incredible sources among Minnesota cops. And his sources were telling him that the guy being hunted down in that parking lot in Miami for the murder of Versace was the same guy police suspected of murdering two men in Minneapolis weeks earlier.

For weeks in 1997 we watched one of the more sensational national manhunts in recent memory—the search for Andrew Cunanan.

There are few things the public—and the press—like more than a good story. ... It's appetite. Your appetite. Our appetite.

What is it about crime stories? It's part fear, part fascination.

Truth isn't just stranger than fiction—it's often more personal ... more relevant ... more compelling than fiction.

Maybe examining who we are—not—helps us better understand who we are.

Then again ... maybe ... we just like a good read. ⚖

Rick Kupchella, Anchor, KARE-11 News, Minneapolis-St. Paul

WANTED

JOHN HERBERT DILLINGER

On June 22, 1934, HOMER S. CUMMINGS, Attorney General of the United States, under the authority vested in him by an Act of Congress approved June 6, 1934, offered a reward of

$10,000.00

for the capture of John Herbert Dillinger or a reward of

$5,000.00

for information leading to the arrest of John Herbert Dillinger.

DESCRIPTION

Age, 32 years; Height, 5 foot 7-1/8 inches; Weight, 153 pounds; Build, medium; Hair, medium chestnut; Eyes, grey; Complexion, medium; Occupation, machinist; Marks and scars, 1/2 inch scar back left hand, scar middle upper lip, brown mole between eyebrows.

All claims to any of the aforesaid rewards and all questions and disputes that may arise as among claimants to the foregoing rewards shall be passed upon by the Attorney General and his decisions shall be final and conclusive. The right is reserved to divide and allocate portions of any of said rewards as between several claimants. No part of the aforesaid rewards shall be paid to any official or employee of the Department of Justice.

If you are in possession of any information concerning the whereabouts of John Herbert Dillinger, communicate immediately by telephone or telegraph collect to the nearest office of the Division of Investigation, United States Department of Justice, the local addresses of which are set forth on the reverse side of this notice.

JOHN EDGAR HOOVER, DIRECTOR,
DIVISION OF INVESTIGATION,
UNITED STATES DEPARTMENT OF JUSTICE,
WASHINGTON, D. C.

June 20, 1934

Gangsters in the Streets
Crooks and Corruption in the Capital City

Of all the Midwest cities, the one I knew best was St. Paul, and it was a crooks' haven. Every criminal of any importance in the 1930s made his home at one time or another in St. Paul. If you were looking for a guy you hadn't seen for a few months, you usually thought of two places—prison or St. Paul.

–Alvin "Creepy" Karpis, in his 1971 autobiography,
Public Enemy Number One: The Alvin Karpis Story

Once upon a time, Minnesota's saintly city was anything but. In the shadow of the lofty state capitol building and the revered Cathedral of St. Paul, the nation's most notorious gangsters roamed freely, welcomed by St. Paul's finest with open arms and promises of safe harbor. The capital of Minnesota Nice was, in fact, one of the nation's top three headquarters for the underworld.

Public enemies rubbed elbows with ordinary citizens, harbored by a corrupt police department in exchange for a promise to commit no crime within city limits. The list of mobsters operating out of St. Paul was like a Who's Who of the nation's most famous criminals—John Dillinger, "Baby Face" Nelson, Alvin "Creepy" Karpis, the Barkers (Ma, Doc and Fred), "Machine Gun" Kelly, Verne Miller, Fred Goetz and more.

How did this all come to pass in seemingly serene and pious St. Paul?

Long before the gangster era, in the late-1800s St. Paul residents demanded that city officials do something to curb a four-year crime spree, according to St. Paul Police Department (SPPD) historical records. In June 1900, John J. O'Connor was appointed police chief, and he set about establishing a system for monitoring the activities of "known crooks" and keeping them from crime in his city. In his now-infamous "layover agreement," aka the O'Connor system, Chief O'Connor blatantly put the word out to criminals nationwide they would be welcome to "lay over" in St. Paul, unharmed by law enforcement, if they abided by three simple rules:

1. They would commit no crime within the city limits of St. Paul. (O'Connor didn't care where else they committed crimes, and the hoodlums he harbored could feel free to go to Minneapolis, for example, and do all the robbing and killing and criminalizing they desired. But they were to behave themselves in his city.)

2. Criminals were required to "check in" with the police department or a go-between when they came to town and to identify themselves so the police would know they were there. And they would then be left alone.

3. It was expected they would make a "donation" to the police department.

"Many St. Paul residents lauded this policy, feeling that it afforded them a safer place to live and work," reports *Saint Paul Police Department: A Historical Review 1854-2000*, a 2000 publication of the SPPD. "According to the police department's 1919 history, this system documented those criminals who were not being pursued by other police departments."

Word spread that St. Paul was a safe haven for all criminals; incredibly, it remained so for about 36 years. But it wasn't until midway through that period, 1919, that St. Paul rose to prominence on the gangland map. That's when Minnesota congressman and former Granite Falls mayor Andrew Volstead wrote his Volstead Act, aka the National Prohibition Act, which single-handedly gave birth to the gangster era. In 1920, Prohibition became law throughout the country. Suddenly, everyone wanted a drink, and bootleggers sprang up everywhere, with gangsters leading the way. Seemingly overnight, trafficking in illegal alcohol was a booming business; small-time hoods became major players; and police departments including St. Paul were in cahoots with crooks.

O'Connor left the SPPD in 1920. In the decade that followed, seven police chiefs were appointed. At times, officers did not know who was chief until they arrived for duty. St. Paul politics would continue to control who held the position of chief until 1936, according to SPPD records.

In 1922 new St. Paul Police Chief Michael Gebhardt estimated that 75 percent of the city's residents were making wine or moonshine. (Minneapolis residents were not exempt. In 2007, 98-year-old Linnea Gordon told *Star Tribune* writer Bill Ward she and her husband made and sold moonshine at her parents' Minneapolis home, doing a thriving business and consorting with other underground characters, including Isadore "Kid Cann" Blumenfeld. They did brisk business out of their home on Friday nights and Saturdays. "We had customers all day, and from all over the place," she told Ward.)

Meanwhile, gangsters flocked to Minnesota. In 1922 Al Creepy Karpis, Doc and Freddie Barker and Kate (Ma) Barker rented a cottage in Mahtomedi and were said to frequent Dick's Inn. ("Residents found them quiet, well mannered and bill paying. When the FBI began making inquiries, the gang made a quiet departure," according to the Washington County Historical Society website.)

Chicago mobsters were known to hang out around White Bear, Big Marine and Forest lakes. While John Dillinger and Baby Face Nelson were renting cottages at nearby Big Marine Lake, the Barker gang occupied one of the cottages behind the Forest Theatre. Several gangsters were known to occupy the Smith cottages on the east side of Forest Lake. (One time, reports the Washington County Historical society website, "George Ruggles was taken at gunpoint from his home to his office, where he was forced to remove a bullet from one of the Barker-Karpis gang members.")

But it was in the city of St. Paul where gangsters reigned as kings, elevated to star status by Prohibition and the O'Connor system. "In the 1920s and 1930s, word had spread around the country that Saint Paul was a safe haven for all criminals. O'Connor's system of 'organized crime with organized intelligence,' which had protected St. Paul residents in earlier years, backfired. St. Paul acted like a magnet, attracting the most notorious gangsters," according to the SPPD historical review. "Those gangsters who came to town lived freely and openly, committing their crimes in other Minnesota towns and neighboring states. Newspapers reported that witnesses who were asked which way the criminals went often said, 'They headed toward St. Paul.' "

But that was OK with the good citizens of St. Paul. In the 1920s and early-1930s, residents and businesses remained relatively untouched, and very few saw bootlegging as a crime. (In fact, Prohibition was not a nice thing to do to good Germans in this hotbed of beer production. In 1887, Minnesota ranked 20th in the nation in state population, but fifth in the nation in beer production, reports the Master Brewers Assoc. on its website. St. Paul was the top brewing center in the state.)

In the midst of Prohibition, in 1925, St. Paul and San Francisco were named the two "wettest" cities in the nation, according to a *Collier's* magazine survey. The Roaring '20s was a glamorous time in St. Paul, when citizens looked to the flamboyantly dressed gangsters as folk heroes akin to Robin Hood. Government took away their liquor. The gangsters brought it back. Speakeasies popped up, and the biggest names in music came to town to play Twin Cities clubs. Local nightlife teemed with color—fedora-topped criminals and their dazzling molls holding forth as the flashy celebrities of the day. For about 15 years, gangsters ruled St. Paul, and storybook criminal names peppered local conversations. (Andrew Volstead, sitting in his office in the Federal Courts Building, now Landmark Center, had a front-row seat to the action.)

But that was the "movie star" side of the story. As years progressed, things would turn ugly, and St. Paul's reputation would be tarnished for years. Yet there are Minnesotans who have lived in the Twin Cities their entire lives and have never heard of gangster crime in their midst. Records were reportedly destroyed or disappeared in both St. Paul and Minneapolis police departments, as they did in law enforcement agencies across the country. (St. Paul was not the only "safe city" in the country.)

Minnesota author Paul Maccabee deserves credit for unearthing Minnesota's gangster history and shining light on St. Paul's unsavory past. His definitive book on the subject, *John Dillinger Slept Here: A Crook's Tour of Crime and Corruption in St. Paul, 1920-1936*, is the culmination of 13 years of research and it remains the bible of St. Paul gangster studies. He conducted hundreds of interviews, and pored over 100,000 pages of FBI files to piece together local history that would otherwise remain buried. In his foreword, Maccabee eloquently answers the question, "Why is historical record of Minnesota's racketeers worth saving? Because, the story of Minneapolis and St. Paul, like that of any city, is a mingling of glory and infamy, of people with high integrity and others with low morals. St. Paul was built as much on a legacy of gamblers, scoundrels and sinners as on a tradition of philanthropists, statesmen and business barons."

The line between "good guys" and "bad guys" was murky back then, and many citizens participated in unlawful activities. In his book, Maccabee details the "intertwining of St. Paul's underworld and overworld" at venues such as Nina Clifford's brothel on South Washington Street, where, legend has it, there was a tunnel from the brothel to the former Minnesota Club, esteemed gathering place for city fathers. ("The story went there were three important people in St. Paul," said reporter Fred Heaberlin in the Maccabee book. "They were James J. Hill, Archbishop John Ireland and Nina

Clifford.") Down the street, at the saloon and brothel Buck
of Blood, the police chief's wife, Annie O'Connor, was the
madam who ran the prostitute ring, according to an O'Connor
descendant and SPPD history.

Linking the police to the gangsters were the "fixers."
In 1928 "Dapper Dan" Hogan, owner of the Green Lantern
speakeasy in St. Paul, acting as the go-between for St. Paul
police and visiting criminals, was killed by a car bomb in his
garage. "The Irish Godfather" was known nationally to settle
mobsters' feuds and launder money. He was succeeded in his
role by Harry Sawyer, who inherited both the Green Lantern
and the O'Connor system. Under Sawyer's reign, St. Paul's
safe haven status for criminals flourished. If a raid was in the
offing, police called to alert the criminals. Sawyer knew such
things as where gangsters could get a getaway car serviced,
and connected people however he could. "Sawyer ran the
Green Lantern like a host at a great party," Karpis wrote in
his autobiography. "The greatest blowout Sawyer threw in
the place, in my experience, was on New Year's Eve, 1932. ...
There was probably never before as complete a gathering of
criminals in one room in the United States as there was at the
Green Lantern that night. There were escapees from every
major U.S. penitentiary. I was dazzled."

In 1930, after release from prison, bootlegging kingpin
Leon Gleckman set up headquarters in the Hotel St. Paul,
which gained fame as a rendezvous for gangsters.

By this time, St. Paul had come under the watchful
eye of J. Edgar Hoover, who had been hired in the mid-'20s to
clean up a corrupt FBI. There was plenty to watch: In the '30s,

the gangs were all here, flaunting their presence and plotting bigger crimes—the Barker-Karpis gang, John Dillinger, Baby Face Nelson, Bugs Moran, Machine Gun Kelly, Homer Van Meter and more.

In 1932 (the same year the Barker-Karpis gang holed up in a rental house on South Robert Street, posing as musicians and carrying violin cases for their "gigs" and driving the unsuspecting landlady's granddaughter to school), things began to change as Prohibition repeal approached. Gangsters had to find new ways to earn money. With no bootlegging to do, their crimes turned violent—to armed robbery, kidnapping and murder. (In 1933, a speaker at the Minnesota Bankers Assoc. annual meeting noted that 21 percent of all bank holdups the previous year occurred in Minnesota—43 robberies totaling $1.39 million, according to *John Dillinger Slept Here*.) Bank guards began to be instructed to shoot to kill.

In December 1932, the Barker-Karpis gang killed two policemen and one bystander in a raid on Third Northwestern National Bank in Minneapolis. In March 1933, Prohibition was repealed (and Volstead himself returned to Granite Falls, where he resumed private law practice). In August 1933, the Barker-Karpis gang killed another police officer and wounded one after robbing the $33,000 stockyards payroll delivered to South St. Paul Post Office.

As Minnesotans watched violent crimes committed against their neighbors, the romantic notions of gangster heroes vanished. They got angry and began calling for justice. There were Tommy guns in the streets. (The brainchild of General John T. Thompson, who was inspired by the trench warfare of World War I to develop the first handheld machine gun, Thompson submachine guns were for sale on the open market. But it was the crooks, not police, who could afford them. In a 1979 interview with a St. Paul Police Department historian, Detective Herbert W. Scott, SPPD patrolman and detective in the 1930s, recalls that the Tommy guns did not come into service in the SPPD until around 1934, after Shreve Archer [head of Archer-Daniels Midland Linseed Co.] bought six of them for the department.)

And suddenly, the last straw: The crooks violated the layover agreement. The Barker-Karpis gang kidnapped two prominent St. Paul millionaires—Edward Bremer of the Bremer Bank, and William Hamm of the Hamm Brewery—in the city of St. Paul. It was the beginning of the end. The kidnappings occurred only six months apart, Hamm snatched in June 1933 for a $100,000 ransom, and Bremer in January 1934 for $200,000.

It was a bad time for kidnapping. The kidnapping death of aviation hero Charles Lindbergh's son in 1932 still lingered in the news. The father of the Barker gang's second kidnap victim was a friend and political donor to President Franklin Roosevelt, who mentioned the kidnapping in one of his radio fireside chats. The crimes brought the Feds into the city, and a cry went out for local police reform.

Violence continued. John Dillinger machine-gunned his way out of an apartment near Lexington and Grand, escaping from the Feds and local police. In March 1934, henchmen for Baby Face Nelson mowed down local resident Theodore Kidder at the corner of Excelsior and Brookside,

according to the St. Louis Park Historical Society website.
Bullet holes were embedded in the stucco and were evident
for many years. (St. Louis Park was becoming known as "Little
Cicero," after the working class suburb of Chicago where
Al Capone moved his gang in 1923 to escape reformers,
according to the website.) Howard Guilford of the *Twin City
Reporter* was shot and killed in September 1934.

Also in 1934, witnesses saw three men gunned down in
front of the fireplace in the Castle Royal, a speakeasy in what is
now the Wabasha Street Caves, but by the time police arrived,
the bodies were gone and the blood cleaned up.

The most notorious death was that of Walter W.
Liggett, editor of the weekly paper *The Midwest American*,
who had reported on links between area gangsters and the
governor of Minnesota, Floyd B. Olson. In December 1935,
Liggett was shot in the alley behind his home, his wife and
daughter witnesses. Kid Cann was indicted by a grand jury but
wasn't convicted.

The Feds were on a mission from 1934 to 1936. FBI
agents were finally granted permission to carry weapons
and make arrests. They did both with a vengeance, and the
gangsters were cut down. John Dillinger was shot to death by
agents in Chicago. Bonnie and Clyde, Baby Face Nelson, and
Pretty Boy Floyd were all killed in shootouts. Ma and Freddie
Barker were gunned down by FBI bullets in 1935 in Florida.
Doc Barker died in 1939 trying to escape from Alcatraz. In
1936, Karpis pled guilty to kidnapping and received a life
sentence in federal prison. He was the last Public Enemy to
be captured. (He would go on to stay at Alcatraz a little over

25 years, longer than any other inmate interned there. After he was paroled in 1969, having served 33 years of a life sentence for the Hamm kidnapping, Karpis completed his autobiography in 1971. He died in 1979.)

In the mid-'30s, headlines in the *Saint Paul Daily News* demanded a cleanup of the St. Paul Police Department, according to SPPD history. The newspaper fired accusations at the police department, charging it with corruption. In 1935, after months of inquiry, 13 members of the SPPD were suspended or fired for corrupt activities, including Police Chief Michael J. Culligan. Under a new administration, the St. Paul Police Department began to rebuild the department and its image in the late-'30s and '40s.

Across the river, the city of Minneapolis also faced a cleanup task. In the mid-'40s, new Minneapolis Mayor Hubert H. Humphrey had his work cut out for him in the city where Isadore (Kid Cann) Blumenfeld reigned as the most notorious mobster in Minnesota, overseeing illegal activities such as bootlegging, prostitution and labor racketeering. Blumenfeld allegedly paid off police and city officials, and a number of deaths are attributed to him. Later, Blumenfeld would also be charged with bankrupting the streetcar system he partially owned in the 1950s. Humphrey hired a new police chief to put an end to corruption and assigned Miles Lord to prosecute mobsters. In a 2007 WCCO-TV interview, Judge Lord said, "The city council was completely beholden to the liquor interest." Humphrey and Lord didn't get Kid Cann, but the Feds did, in 1959, on charges of transporting a prostitute across state lines. After prison he moved to Miami but often visited Minnesota. He died in 1981 and is buried in Edina.

With the gangster era over, the benefit of hindsight had officials wondering if the obsession with this brand of criminals had hindered bigger efforts. "While all eyes were riveted on the blazing chases of Pretty Boy Floyd, Baby Face Nelson et al, the Mafia and its allies were quietly building a criminal cartel preying on the nation," said former FBI agent William Turner in the Maccabee book.

Fast-forward to present, and the passage of time has made old-time gangsters glamorous again. As of this writing, Johnny Depp has announced he will star in a new John Dillinger movie. St. Paul gangster tours do a bustling tourism business, taking visitors via motorcoaches on a historical journey through St. Paul's sordid past, led by costumed gangsters pointing out sites such as Ma Barker's home, Dillinger's apartment, nightclubs and locations of infamous robberies and shootouts. (On at least two occasions, one gangster tour guide reports, the tour bus was stopped by St. Paul Police, who apprehended the guide and confiscated the "Tommy gun" after responding to concerned citizen reports that someone was holding a bus full of senior citizens hostage at gunpoint.)

Other signs of St. Paul's gangster past linger. In the fireplace room at Wabasha Street Caves, which is now a venue for special events, tour guides point out bullet holes left by a gangland hit when the room was part of the Castle Royal speakeasy. Over the years, employees and visitors have repeatedly reported ghost sightings there, telling of ghostly gangsters, or of big band music when no band was playing. Mists have shown up in wedding photos taken in the caves, and employees have reported seeing strange globes of light floating around the bar area.

That's not the only gangster ghost sighting in town. Downtown, the ghost of Jack Peifer is said to haunt Landmark Center, the former Minnesota Federal Courthouse, where Peifer was tried and sentenced to 30 years for his part in the kidnapping of William Hamm by the Barker gang. In 1936, he committed suicide in his cell.

Other gangster history lives on in more tangible ways. The St. Paul Police Historical Society talks openly about the O'Connor system and corruption on its website and is looking for a way to put artifacts on display, including a donated 1930s 410-gauge shotgun from the heirs of late FBI agent Sam Hardy, and is documenting oral histories.

St. Paul Police Chief John Harrington told *Star Tribune* reporters in May 2007 he laughs when he hears today's police rookies talk about gang violence as if it were something new in town. "When they go up and see the pictures of Baby Face Nelson and John Dillinger with submachine guns and Colt .45s, it gives them context," the chief told *Star Tribune*. "We've been chasing armed bad guys through the streets for years and we've done it well, and these oral histories can keep those traditions alive." ⚒

Clockwise from top left: Evelyn Frechette (John Dillinger's girlfriend), George "Machine Gun" Kelly and friend, Ma Barker (here with husband George, who left after the birth of their last son) and Alvin "Creepy" Karpis all operated in the St. Paul area during the gangster era.

The home of William Hamm Jr. on St. Paul's east side just after his kidnapping in June 1933 by the Barker-Karpis gang. Mobster speakeasy The Castle Royal is now The Wabasha Street Caves, across the Wabasha Bridge from downtown St. Paul.
(photo: Minnesota Historical Society)

Reporters gather outside the West Seventh Street St. Paul home of banker Edward
Bremer after his abduction by the Barker-Karpis gang in 1934.
(photo: Minnesota Historical Society)

The former Bremer home today.

Baby Face Nelson (Lester Gillis) wanted poster.

George "Bugs" Moran was born in St. Paul and became an archenemy of Al Capone in Chicago.

Modern-day photo of Brookside and Excelsior Boulevard in St. Louis Park, site of the Baby Face Nelson gang's shooting of Theodore Kidder in 1934.

Isadore "Kid Cann" Blumenfeld reigned as the most notorious mobster in Minnesota.

Edith Liggett awaits proceedings during the 1936 trial for her husband's murder in Minneapolis.

Kid Cann on trial for the murder of Walter Liggett. (photos: Minnesota Historical Society)

The FBI's J. Edgar Hoover kept close watch over Minnesota gangsters.

Jack Peifer, who owned a speakeasy on Mississippi River Boulevard, is said to haunt The Landmark Center (lower right), which was formerly the Federal Courts Building in St. Paul.

The St. Paul Hotel hosted mob bosses in the '30s.

The Landmark Center in St. Paul was the Federal Courthouse in the 1930s.

Carol Thompson, 1928 -1963. (inset photo: Minnesota Historical Society)

The Murder of Carol Thompson
When the Unthinkable Happened in Highland Park

It was March 6, 1963 in St. Paul. The state's capital city was in the last days of a Minnesota winter. On Hillcrest Avenue in the Highland Park neighborhood, Ruth Nelson opened her door just after 9 a.m. to find her 34-year-old neighbor, Carol Thompson, on her doorstep wearing a blue robe and covered with blood. Across the street, the Pearsons were watching, and Dr. Fritz Pearson rushed over to help. Carol had multiple stab wounds and a knife stuck in her throat. She could speak, but barely. "A man came to the door ..." she whispered before she collapsed. To Pearson, who administered first aid, she said, "I got a knife stuck in my throat." Rushed to Ancker Hospital, Carol Thompson died on the operating table at 12:58 p.m. The Ramsey County coroner said she had a skull fracture, brain hemorrhage, contusion of the brain and two stab wounds in her neck, plus 25 separate cuts on her head caused by a blunt object.

At first, the police had no clues. It seemed completely out of character for this horrible attack and murder to have happened to this woman in this neighborhood of the city.

Carol Thompson was a wife and mother, married to up-and-coming young lawyer T. Eugene Thompson. The couple had four young children: a boy, Jeffrey, 13, and three younger daughters. Thompson had a busy downtown practice and was chair of the Criminal Law Committee for the Minnesota Bar Assoc. The couple had been married for 15 years.

Although the late 1960s were a time of major protest in America, in 1963 the war in Vietnam was just heating up. John and Jackie Kennedy were the glamorous first couple; Karl Rolvaag was Minnesota's governor; Coach Norm Van Brocklin and his "scrambling quarterback" Fran Tarkenton were approaching the Minnesota Vikings' third season; and The Tyrone Guthrie Theater would have its first performance in June.

In this upper middle class neighborhood, husbands went to work and wives stayed home to manage the family. The Thompsons were no exception. Carol sewed, making all her own and her daughters' clothes; T. Eugene (while small and somewhat unprepossessing) was known as a snappy and expensive dresser. Such an event in this seemingly perfect family was unfathomable.

As the word got out that afternoon, a pall of fear crept over St. Paul's neighborhoods. Husbands made sure family doors were locked and that wives and children were home safe. Doors were not opened except to known visitors—perhaps some kind of homicidal maniac was on the loose.

From the beginning, the police work was meticulous. Detectives looked first at the husband but moved on. Pretty and popular Carol Thompson had an admirer, some thought. A window and doors salesman nicknamed Big Red was said to have been infatuated with her, although Carol herself had put a stop to it. Upon investigation, Big Red had an air-tight alibi. The police kept looking.

Then they got lucky. Police reports show that an anonymous call came in stating that it was well known that T. Eugene had a mistress and was a spender. The investigation turned again to T. Eugene and things began to unravel fast. They found petite Jackie Oleson who had been keeping company with T. Eugene for the better part of a year between her marriages, traveling with him and even working in his law office for a time.

When a police press conference displayed fragments of a handmade gun handle found at the scene, another anonymous call came in about a stolen Luger pistol with a handmade handle. Tips rolled in to the police. The gun had been seen in the possession of a small-time thug and sometime boxer named Norman Mastrian. Mastrian had been heard shopping around a contract for a "hit" on a St. Paul woman. Leads went from one hood to another, ending at Dick W.C. Anderson, who was picked up in Phoenix. It didn't take long for Anderson to talk, his story being that Mastrian paid him $3,000 to commit the murder; the scene was prepped and details were provided that could only have come from one source, Thompson himself. Almost immediately, police learned that several insurance policies totaling $1.6 million had been purchased on Carol's life during the 12 months before the murder, the last policy having been bought just two months previously.

In his confession, Anderson said Mastrian provided him a floor plan of the house on Hillcrest Avenue, and told him the side door would be open—evidently a standard practice of the family. At 9 a.m. the children would be at school. T. Eugene, whose regular habit was to arrive at his office after 10, according to his staff, left much earlier that morning, dropping son Jeffrey off at St. Paul Academy on the way. The family dog had recently been given away, and the only phone in the house was now in the kitchen according to a story in the *St. Paul Dispatch*, March 1963. This was the second morning the same plan was in effect, as Anderson said he had gotten cold feet the previous day. On March 6, fortified by vodka, Anderson testified that he entered the house by the side door, waiting in the basement for Carol to answer her husband's phone call in the kitchen. Following her upstairs, he confronted her in her bed, where she was reading. He was supposed to knock her out with a rubber hose and then drown her in the bathtub, which had been partially filled in readiness. But Carol was a fighter. She came to after the first blows, and a terrible fight ensued all over the house. The Luger that Mastrian gave Anderson didn't fire, so he beat Carol with it, finally stabbing her in the neck with a kitchen knife. He then went back upstairs to wash himself up and make the scene look like a robbery, thinking she was dead. Improbably, Carol got to her feet and staggered out the side door, leaving a bloody trail outside two other homes before collapsing at the Nelson's.

Thompson had resumed much of his way of life after the murder. The evening of Carol's funeral he was seen out to dinner at the Lexington, a popular St. Paul restaurant. The children (William Swanson documented their experiences in his book *Dial M: The Murder of Carol Thompson*) went back to school and picked up their lives, cared for at first by relatives and then by a loving housekeeper. Thompson's behavior involved more fast living and even women coming to the house, said observers. Then on June 21, Thompson

was arrested. He hired well-known attorneys Hy Segell and
Bill Fallon to put on a vigorous defense. Even with the "other
woman" motive, a conviction wasn't assured. With no previous
record, Thompson was a respected member of the community;
much of the evidence was circumstantial and attested to only
by criminal low-life associates of Mastrian.

The "murder of the century" the newspapers
called it. For the trial, which began on October 28, 1963 in
Minneapolis (after a change of venue), reporters were on
hand from newspapers including the *New York Times* and the
Chicago Daily News. Local papers sent Al McConagha leading
the *Minneapolis Morning Tribune* team; Don Giese for the *St.
Paul Pioneer Press/Dispatch*; and Larry Fitzmaurice for the
Minneapolis Star. Young reporter Barbara Flanagan was to
provide "color" for the *Star*.

Dick W.C. Anderson's testimony regarding the blow-
by-blow details of the crime itself was horrendous. Asked if
Carol said anything through this ordeal he related that at one
point she did say, "Oh God, help me," whereupon Thompson
collapsed at the defense table.

The testimony of the mistress, 27-year-old Mrs.
Jackie Oleson, was highly anticipated. According to reports
in the Star, Oleson "poured out a tale of extramarital
intrigue, an offer of marriage and a proposed Thompson
gift of $10,000." She admitted a long relationship with
Thompson at various locations throughout the state. Oleson
was described as a petite brunette, wearing a "black sheath
dress trimmed with black fur," according to a November
1963 *Minneapolis Star* story.

Then-reporter Barbara Flanagan watched it all. Asked for her impressions of T. Eugene she said, "He was Mister Big Shot, treating reporters and others to lunch at Charlie's Restaurant every day of the trial. He seemed almost thrilled by his notoriety. I never went to one of those lunches," she said in an interview in October 2007.

After Oleson's testimony, Barbara went further. She and photographer Gerald Brimacombe knocked on the door at Jackie's home. The elusive mistress gave them a long, exclusive interview that scooped every other reporter on the story. ("It was one of the high points of my career," said Flanagan.)

"Don't think I'm the only woman," Oleson told Flanagan, as she described growing up in foster homes. "Gene Thompson was the only security I ever knew," she said tearfully. "Was I in love with him? Oh, yes."

The trial went on, claiming front-page news daily except for three days beginning Nov. 22, 1963, when President Kennedy was assassinated. The entire country came to a halt, but T. Eugene's trial went on. Ramsey County prosecutor William Randall cited key links to Thompson's guilt—among them, the removal of the family dog, supposedly due to some redecorating; Thompson's early arrival at his office on the two mornings in question; the partially pre-filled bathtub; the insurance policies on Carol's life; and Jackie Oleson, whom Randall said Thompson wanted to marry. Thompson's testimony on the stand didn't help him—he was unconvincing. Though he admitted his infidelities, he maintained he had confessed them to his wife and denied any culpability in her murder. The verdict came back in one day—Thompson was convicted of first-degree murder and sentenced to life in prison. A few months later, Mastrian was also convicted. Both men were in Stillwater Prison when *Minneapolis Star* columnist Jim Klobuchar spent a week locked up there in 1968 for several articles on life behind bars. First in the series was a piece on T. Eugene Thompson, who discussed maintaining his identity in prison.

"I try to get along," he said, "...you have to look ahead. I mean, you have to keep hoping you're going to find a way out," said Thompson, who admitted to doing some legal counseling for inmates. Klobuchar quotes Thompson as trying to stay a bit detached, as opposed to Mastrian, who is "the happiness boy of the institution, a Kiwanian type among killers, arsonists and thieves." Thompson also tried hard to maintain a relationship with his children, who did visit him occasionally, wrote Klobuchar in the *Minneapolis Star*, June 10, 1968.

After two failed appeals, Thompson served nearly his full sentence at Stillwater Prison and was paroled after 20 years. Mastrian also served a full 20 years in Stillwater. Dick W.C. Anderson, who was removed from Stillwater Prison in fear of his life, completed his sentence at the U.S. Penitentiary in Leavenworth, Kan. Both Thompson and Mastrian are known to reside in the Twin Cities. The current whereabouts of Thompson's former mistress, Jackie Oleson, are unknown.

At age 80, Thompson lives quietly in St. Paul, showing up for jury duty when called (he was excused); trying to regain his law license (it was denied); and even trying to collect

Carol's insurance money. He has a cordial if not effusive relationship with his grown children, who in 1986 conducted a mock re-trial with their father in attendance, reviewing all evidence and testimony, giving him an opportunity to clear himself with them. But their verdict was the same: guilty, said oldest child and only son Jeffrey Thompson in a November 2007 interview.

Jeffrey Thompson became a trial lawyer, then a prosecutor and is now a respected judge in the Third Judicial District in Winona. "I think I decided that the law was important, and if I could learn how the system works I could better protect my family," he says today. Looking back now on his mother's murder, Thompson says, "It's not something you can forget or put aside; it's like losing an arm or a leg—it's always gone and you constantly have to adapt yourself." He sees T. Eugene rarely now—at an occasional Thanksgiving dinner or family event. Has his father ever admitted his role in Carol's murder? "Never," says Judge Thompson. ⚖

The cover of the St. Paul evening daily on the day of the attack. Footprints in the photo show the path of the intruder. (Minnesota Historical Society)

The Thompson house on Hillcrest in St. Paul as police investigate for clues on the day of the attack in 1963. The tree-lined street today.
(photo: Minnesota Historical Society)

St. Paul homicide detective Earl Miels (upper left) arrested T. Eugene Thompson (below) at his Forest Lake cabin. William Randall (upper right) was the Ramsey County prosecutor in the case. Thompson went from grieving husband to suspect to guilty in eight months. (photos: Minnesota Historical Society and AP)

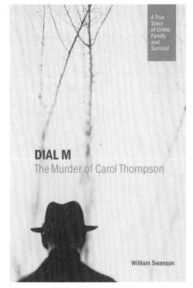

Clockwise from top left: Norman Mastrian and Dick W.C. Anderson were convicted
of murder in the death of Carol Thompson. On Nov. 22, 1963, JFK's assassination
temporarily halted the Thompson trial. Books including *Dial M* by
William Swanson have chronicled the Thompson case.
(photos: Minnesota Historical Society and AP)

Clockwise from top left: T. Eugene Thompson upon parole in 1983; his son Jeffrey Thompson became an attorney then judge. Carol's grave in the mausoleum at Forest Lawn Cemetery in Maplewood. The gravestone reads "Carol Swoboda Thompson 1928-1963."

The Murder of Dennis Jurgens
Lois Jurgens Faces Trial 22 Years Later

When Jerry Puckett was committed to the Home School in Sauk Centre, Minn., as a runaway, she was 16 and pregnant. It was 1961. About that same time, Lois and Harold Jurgens, married and living in White Bear Lake, were trying to adopt a second child. Lois Jurgens wanted the baby to be Catholic, and Jerry had been listed as Catholic in a previous foster home.

But for that twist of fate, the murder of a bright 3-and-a-half-year-old might never have happened. Jerry's son, Dennis, was adopted into the Jurgens home in 1962 and died in 1965. In Dennis Jurgens' short life, he suffered endless beatings, force feedings, severe pain, bruising and more, amounting to outrageous and brutal treatment at the hands of his adoptive mother that led to his tragic and tortured death. His death was listed as peritonitis, stemming from a ruptured bowel, which could only have been caused from some sort of sharp blow.

At the time, there was no serious investigation into Dennis' death. Not from the county coroner who wrote "deferred" in the box for accident, suicide or homicide on the death certificate. Not from the police in White Bear Lake. (Lois' brother was a police lieutenant in the department and reputedly soft-pedaled the investigation.) Not from the social worker, who later said she had bad feelings about placing Dennis with the Jurgens, but ultimately approved the adoption. And not from the many family members, neighbors and friends who witnessed Lois seriously abusing the child and did nothing, said nothing. The investigation closed and Dennis was buried, although the two policemen on the case were so sufficiently disturbed that they immediately removed an older adopted boy, Robert, from the Jurgens' home. This information was only revealed 21 years later when Lois Jurgens was indicted for Dennis' death, according to the *Minneapolis Star and Tribune* and the *St. Paul Pioneer Press and Dispatch.*

The indictment and subsequent trial came about because Dennis' birth mother, Jerry (now) Sherwood, single-handedly forced a re-opening of the case in 1986. As she searched for answers about her son's death, she found the word "deferred" on the death certificate and enough other documentation to question the first examiner's report. Reviewing autopsy reports and photos made it clear to Ramsey County medical examiner Dr. Michael McGee that Dennis had been severely beaten, and McGee re-classified the death as a homicide.

Reporter Brian Bonner broke the story of Jerry's quest in the *Pioneer Press and Dispatch* on Oct. 12, 1986. "She's the real hero," McGee told Bonner. "I realized it was one of those cases where no one wanted to make up their mind." The homicide classification triggered a new police investigation, and in January 1987, 21 years after Dennis' death, Lois Jurgens was indicted on second- and third-degree murder charges.

And so, this is a parallel story of two women whose lives came unhappily together over the desperate fate of one doomed little boy.

Lois Jurgens was raised as one of 16 children in the Zerwas family. As Barry Siegel's book, *A Death in White Bear*

Lake, documents, it was known that her father didn't work and was often rough and abusive. The family scraped by financially, doing slightly better once the older children could work and contribute to the family coffers. Children, and lots of children, were expected in this large, Catholic family. Lois married Harold Jurgens, an only child of doting parents. Harold, who was musical and had a band at one time, settled down to work as an electrician once he married.

Though the marriage seemed to take, Lois did not get pregnant, telling friends and family that Harold was sterile. Lois was dominant in the marriage, with Harold usually going along, wrote Siegel. In 1960, the couple privately adopted Robert, who was a quiet child. Before long, Lois wanted another child—a baby, she said. The search was lengthy because of the request for a Catholic child. Finally, Lutheran Social Services matched them with almost 1-year-old Dennis, listed as Catholic at birth. Although the social worker on the case had vague concerns about whether or not the Jurgens really wanted Dennis, the placement was made.

In contrast to Robert, who was two years older, bright and personable, Dennis was much more active. He wasn't easy for Lois to control and, relatives testified at her trial, her methods were more than harsh. Eight months after the adoption, Dennis was hospitalized with a severe scalding to his penis and scrotum. Lois maintained he had turned the hot water faucet onto himself. No investigation took place even after the doctor on the case, Dr. Roy Peterson, reported his suspicions, the doctor testified at the trial. Ultimately skin grafts were not needed and Dennis went home with Lois.

As reported in both the *Star and Tribune* and *Pioneer Press and Dispatch,* Lois was determined to mold Dennis into the child she wanted, like the quieter Robert. She obsessed about his weight (which was normal for his age) and began to starve him, to get rid of "sloppy fat," as she called it. Lois' brother and sister testifying at her trial spoke of Lois force-feeding Dennis horseradish and his own vomit when he wouldn't eat, wrote the *Star Tribune.* She placed a clothespin on his penis to keep him from wetting the bed. She would tie him to the toilet to force a bowel movement. Another relative told how Lois tied him spread-eagled to his crib so he wouldn't mess up his room. His ears were torn from being lifted by them; he was afraid to cry and would only whimper. Lois made him wear sunglasses to cover up his frequently black eyes. At age 3, he was forced to memorize the rosary by "making him kneel on a broomstick," *Star and Tribune* cited relatives as reporting. Final examination of his severely bruised body showed many bite marks on his genitalia.

Reportedly, Harold Jurgens was not abusive to Dennis himself but didn't intervene. Before the trial, several relatives claimed Lois threatened to kill them if they testified, whereupon the judge delivered Lois a sharp reprimand. All of this information as revealed in the trial was reported daily by both the *Star and Tribune* and the *Pioneer Press and Dispatch.*

Star Tribune writer Dennis Cassano reported on the older brother's trial testimony as Robert, now a police officer in Crookston, described his brother's brutal treatment. As a terrified 5-year-old, he recalled seeing Dennis tumbling down a flight of stairs as if he were thrown, after which his mother struck and shook him. He remembered her often submerging 3-and-a-half-year-old Dennis' head in water as he gasped for air. On the night Dennis died, Robert testified he walked into his brother's room "just as she was picking him up out of the crib ... Dennis' body just kind of draped ... he was just dangling. She began to violently shake Dennis and holler his name. There was no response."

When interviewed in 1987, Dennis' natural mother, Jerry Sherwood, told the *Star and Tribune* she was a confused, unwed teenager when she had to give up her baby shortly after his December 1961 birth. Growing up without a mother, her life had been riddled with stepmothers, foster homes and insecurities. A ward of the state, Jerry bounced in and out of the Home School, which eventually provided her some sense of security.

Although she went on to have three daughters and another son (whom she also named Dennis) with the first baby's father, Dennis McIntyre, subsequently marrying him, she never forgot this first child. Finally in 1980, after a divorce from McIntyre, and another marriage and divorce, the now Jerry Sherwood decided to find her first-born. An inquiry to the county elicited the response that her son had died in 1965, but, saying she had given up her legal rights, gave no other information. Devastated, Jerry Sherwood said she let the fact of her son's death fester for six years. Suddenly in 1986, she told *Pioneer Press and Dispatch*'s Brian Bonner, she decided to find his grave.

Reviewing the death records in the attending mortuary, Sherwood discovered a yellowed clipping headlining the toddler's death, reported Bonner in his article. In discussing the autopsy results, the documents stated that in addition to the ruptured bowel and subsequent peritonitis, "the body also bore multiple injuries and bruises." At that moment, Jerry Sherwood became a mother fiercely defending her young. She went to the police, insisting the case be re-opened.

Heated grand jury and later trial testimony argued whether the ruptured bowel could have resulted from Dennis' fall down the stairs. As reported in the *Star Tribune*, pediatrician Dr. E. Dale Cumming testified it would take considerable force—such as the impact of a high-speed traffic accident—and that very seldom could a fall cause a bowel to rupture." Prosecutors said no one but Lois could have caused the injury, the newspaper's reporting continued.

Jerry Sherwood attended every day of the trial. Lois Jurgens, defended by highly experienced defense attorney Doug Thomson, did not testify, nor did her husband Harold, who was not granted immunity. (Harold Jurgens had testified under immunity to the grand jury, however.) Opposing Thomson were two young prosecuting attorneys in the Ramsey County attorney's office—Clayton Robinson Jr. and Melinda Elledge.

Thomson's approach admitted the abuse (too difficult to deny) but took the position that it did not cause the child's death. The jury didn't buy it, and in just five hours found her guilty of third-degree murder (killing without intent), dismissing the second-degree charge of intentional murder.

Now began the second or sanity phase of the trial. Thomson presented professional psychiatrists to testify that Lois was insane. Dr. James Stephans said she was a paranoid schizophrenic and met the definition of criminally insane. (Lois Jurgens had a record of depression and had been medicated over the years.) The jury found this testimony inconsistent with that given by witnesses in the first part of the trial and on June 5, 1987 declared her to be sane. The judge immediately sentenced Lois Jurgens, now 61, to up to 25 years in prison.

Jerry Sherwood was jubilant about the length of the sentence. "Dennis would have been 25 years old in December, and she got 25 years. I'm so happy," said Sherwood as she was interviewed on television. She kept saying over and over, "25 years, 25 years."

In sentencing Jurgens, Ramsey County Chief Judge David Marsten said that she was guilty of acts of cruelty of "barbaric proportions" because of her abuse of her young son, who was in a position of "extreme vulnerability," reported the *Star and Tribune*.

The two prosecuting attorneys were ecstatic about the verdict. "I think I'll wake up tomorrow and say, 'Damn, we did it,' " Robinson told the *Star and Tribune*. "In 1965, I didn't think ... middle-class families on a nice tree-lined street would murder their children," Elledge told the *Star and Tribune*. Family members who had spoken out felt vindicated. The *Star and Tribune* reported that jury foreman John W. Johnson said of the verdict: "The child was battered beyond belief; it was impossible to come to any other conclusion ... she just destroyed him."

Robert Jurgens was also heralded for his bravery in testifying against his mother. Though he had been removed from the Jurgens at age 5, he was returned later. (The Jurgens

later adopted four siblings from Kentucky, who were also
abused by Lois and later removed.)

Jurgens was now a convicted murderer, guilty of
killing Dennis Jurgens after two years of brutal abuse. Doug
Thomson's efforts for an appeal were all rejected. However,
just eight years later in 1995, Jurgens was released due to an
indeterminate sentencing law then in place. Contacted in
Denver where she now lived, Jerry Sherwood was irate. "How
can you take a boy's life like that, beat it for two years and then
walk free?" Sherwood asked. "May God strike her dead, that's
what I have to say to Lois Jurgens," Sherwood told *Star and
Tribune* reporters.

After the trial and sentence, life in White Bear Lake
settled down. In 1988 Diane Sawyer did a 60 Minutes report,
"No One Saved Dennis." Barry Siegel's book was published in
1990. NBC produced a television movie, *A Child Lost Forever*,
in 1992, telling the story from Jerry Sherwood's perspective
and starring Beverly D'Angelo as Jerry. Harold Jurgens died
in 2000; the police investigated his death because of Lois
Jurgens' past but it was determined he died of a heart attack.
In 2002, the *Pioneer Press* quoted Lois Jurgens in a "Where
Are They Now?" profile as saying she was "living the life of a
homebody." Defense attorney Doug Thomson died in 2007.
Melinda Elledge and Clayton Robinson, Jr. are still with the
Ramsey County attorney's office. Lois Jurgens lives on quietly
in Stillwater, with her pet poodle, tending her roses. ⚖

Harold and Lois Jurgens, here with Dennis Jurgens. (photo: Minnesota Historical Society)

Robert Vander Wyst was a White Bear Lake police officer in the 1960s who had concerns about Dennis Jurgens' case. Upper right: Tom Foley was the Ramsey County District Attorney during the Jurgens trial. Foley later ran for Congress. Bottom: Lois Jurgens leads her attorney, Doug Thomson, and her husband, Harold, into court in 1987.
(photos: Minnesota Historical Society)

The Jurgens trial packed the courtroom at Ramsey County Courthouse in downtown St. Paul in 1987.

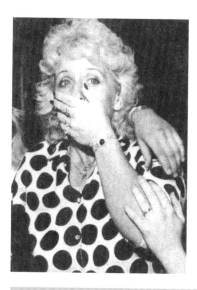

Jurgens guilty of murder

Sanity phase will decide her fate

By Dan Oberdorfer
Staff Writer

More than 22 years after Dennis Jurgens' death, a jury Friday convicted his adoptive mother of murder, deliberating only 3½ hours.

The jury in the oldest homicide case ever tried in Minnesota found that Lois Jurgens, 61, unintentionally killed her adopted son through a brutal pattern of abuse that culminated in his death in April of 1965.

Jurgens was acquitted of a charge of intending to kill the 3½-year-old boy.

Jerry Sherwood, Dennis' birth mother, let out a loud sigh of relief when the guilty verdict was read in a St. Paul courtroom late yesterday afternoon. She and her other children cheered, burst into tears and hugged. "The baby can rest in peace now," Sherwood said.

The verdict means that on Monday a second phase of the trial will begin to determine if Jurgens was insane

Jerry Sherwood reacts to the verdict. The TV movie *A Child Lost Forever* traced the
Dennis Jurgens case. Minnesota newspapers announced the verdict.
(photos: Minnesota Historical Society and *Star Tribune*)

Dennis Jurgens' gravesite at St. Mary's cemetery on the shores of Bald Eagle Lake
near White Bear Lake.

Mrs. Harry Piper, with her husband at her side, spoke with reporters
about her kidnapping. (photo: AP)

The Virginia Piper Kidnapping
Case Unsolved, Million-Dollar Ransom Still Missing

I was absolutely convinced that my client and the co-defendant in that case were absolutely innocent and had been put on trial because the FBI had only two weeks left on a five-year statute of limitations. The FBI wanted to solve what was the biggest kidnapping case—that is, in terms of non-recovered ransom money—in the history of the FBI, a million bucks in 20-dollar bills.

–Ron Meshbesher, defense attorney in the Virginia Piper kidnapping case, *Minnesota Law & Politics*, 2005.

Drive 15 miles west of downtown Minneapolis along Highway 12, and just past Long Lake you'll reach the tony suburb of Orono. Here, stately homes line the north shore of Lake Minnetonka, where in summers, well-heeled residents live a seemingly idyllic resort lifestyle alongside the Twin Cities' largest and most elite lake. It's the perfect setting for a wealthy socialite to take a leisurely stroll on her estate grounds, or perhaps to tend her flowers. That's what 49-year-old Virginia Piper may have been doing one Thursday morning in July when two armed, masked men abducted her in the garden of her Orono home.

On July 27, 1972, the wife of millionaire Harry Piper Jr., board chairman of Minneapolis brokerage firm Piper, Jaffray & Hopwood, was taken by two men described as "heavyset and tough-looking." The thugs walked into her home, taped a housekeeper to a chair and left a note demanding $1 million in ransom, to be paid in $20 bills. They fled in a car shortly after noon, forcing Mrs. Piper to lie on the back seat of their car with a pillowcase over her head while they drove to Jay Cooke State Park near Duluth.

Years later, the Pipers' oldest son, Harry Piper III, in a *Star Tribune* interview recalled how his mother, who was no doubt terrified, "kept her wits about her and was able to get these people to like her enough so that instead of killing her, they returned her alive and basically unharmed. She kept talking, told them about her grandchildren and asked them about whatever she could think of."

After reading the ransom note for his wife, Harry Piper Jr. set out for the money—walking into the office of his neighborhood bank, scrawling out an IOU on a legal pad and leaving with 110 pounds of $20 bills, amounting to $1 million. (He didn't even sign the IOU until several hours after he got the money, according to a 1987 *Star Tribune* story, because George Dixon, the former chairman of First Bank System who then was president of First National Bank of Minneapolis, forgot to ask him for it. "He's a man of great integrity," Dixon told the newspaper reporter. "I had absolutely no qualms about that loan." He was not disappointed; Piper repaid the ransom loan in about three weeks.)

Kidnappers first contacted the family the next night, at 9:30 p.m. Friday, demanding the $1 million. Piper himself delivered the cash—at 11:25 p.m. that same evening, reportedly dropping the money behind a north Minneapolis bar. Piper put it in the trunk of a car and left the car behind a

bar on Plymouth Avenue North. It was at that time the largest
ransom ever reported in the United States, almost double the
previous high of $600,000 delivered for the return of 6-year-old
Bobby Greenlease in 1953 in Missouri.

Richard G. Held, agent in charge of the Minneapolis
FBI office, told a *Star Tribune* reporter that July that FBI agents
found Mrs. Piper through an anonymous call from a third
party who had been contacted by another anonymous caller.
She was found unharmed, but "dirty and rained on," according
to FBI statements, chained to a tree in the Fond du Lac State
Forest area near Duluth, about noon Saturday.

That was in 1972. In the aftermath, wealthy
suburbanites tightened security, shaken by the crime. For
five years the trail was cold, investigators stumped. There was
no suspect, no recovered ransom. Then, in 1977, just as the
statute of limitations on the case was about to expire, Donald
Larson and his business partner, Kenneth Callahan, were
charged with the crime in a case built mainly on a partial
fingerprint and a hair sample. The two men were found guilty
and sentenced to life.

Minneapolis criminal defense attorney Ron
Meshbesher, who represented Callahan, said in a 1988 *Star
Tribune* story he was "convinced they had the wrong people on
trial. The evidence was very weak and my client had a strong
alibi. He was out fishing on Lake Minnetonka at the time of
the kidnapping."

An appeal was made on the grounds that the judge
had improperly barred the testimony of a key defense
witness. Meshbesher recalled the case in a memorable April

2005 interview in *Minnesota Law & Politics*, in which he and attorney Joe Friedberg traded war stories while the tape recorder ran: "The first case resulted in a conviction even though I thought we had it in the bag," said Meshbesher. "The jury was 10-2 for not guilty on the first ballot, and an engineer from IBM in Rochester turned the whole jury around during five days of deliberation. After that I never put an engineer on any jury again. Fortunately, the Court of Appeals granted a new trial in 1979 because the trial judge abused his discretion by refusing to allow the defense to reopen its case to call a vital witness who we were unable to locate until after the parties had rested."

The witness was Linda Billstrom, who told attorney Friedberg: "Those guys didn't do it. I know who did it. My husband and his cohorts did it because I heard them planning it." After the defense attempted to introduce Billstrom as a witness, "Judge Devitt rules that she showed up too late, and then the Eighth Circuit sent it back and said listen to her," said Friedberg in the *Law & Politics* interview.

In the second trial, a fingerprint expert testified that the incriminating print linked to Larson had been altered. "We proved beyond a doubt that the FBI had altered the alleged fingerprint of Larson on a critical piece of evidence," said Meshbesher in *Law & Politics*. "I called a fingerprint expert witness from New York, who showed the jury how the fingerprint was faked." The prosecution did not rebut the claim, and both Callahan and Larson were quickly acquitted.

"And may I say, that was probably the best experience I've ever had representing a defendant," said Meshbesher

in *Law & Politics*. "Sometimes you have a feeling a client
is innocent but you really never know it. I was absolutely
convinced that my client and the co-defendant in that case
were absolutely innocent."

Hennepin County Judge Thor Anderson, who was the
prosecutor in the second trial, in a 2005 *City Pages* interview
said he was surprised by the acquittal, and recalled that the
evidence at the second trial was stronger than in the first.
He called Larson a "vanilla" defendant. "He came across as
an average Joe—kind of like the guy who works for the lawn
service or drives a tow truck."

Virginia Piper herself was certain that Larson and
Callahan were the kidnappers. But Meshbesher maintains
that neither man had anything to do with the crime. He's not
convinced Linda Billstrom's husband did either. "But there
was more evidence against them than on our clients," said
Meshbesher in the 2005 story.

After he was found not guilty, Callahan led a quiet life
in Cumberland, Wis., becoming best friends with the chief
of police there. Callahan died in 2005 after suffering a heart
attack while shoveling snow.

Larson, on the other hand, has won dubious acclaim
as the oldest "lifer" in a Minnesota prison. Even before being
taken in in 1977 for the Piper kidnapping, he was convicted in
1976 and sentenced to life for shooting to death his wife, her
boyfriend and that man's children.

Virginia Piper died of cancer at her home in
Orono in 1988 at age 65. The cancer "was worse than the
kidnapping," her son related in her news obituary. "She

was angry at first and frightened but eventually she battled it. She was courageous and didn't give up." The Virginia Piper Cancer Institute at Abbott Northwestern Hospital in Minneapolis is her legacy. She and Harry were married for 45 years.

In August 1990, her husband, Harry Piper Jr., died of bone cancer at 72.

In 1999, son Harry Piper III sued to gain access to prosecution records that might shed light on the unsolved case. The eldest of Virginia and Harry Jr.'s three sons, Harry III told reporters he would write a book about the crime. After the U.S. attorney's office in Minneapolis responded it couldn't find the case files, Piper (a retired trial attorney turned writer) sued under the Freedom of Information Act and in 2004 won access to 80,000 pages of FBI files relating to the kidnapping, as well as won more than $74,000 in legal costs. But his mother died the day before he was scheduled to interview her about the kidnapping, and his father and other family members were vehemently opposed to the book. So far, a book has not materialized. Maybe someday: Harry III and his wife, Mary, live in Oregon, where, according to a 2008 charity bio, "he does a little writing and a lot of fishing these days."

The case was never solved. The ransom money is still missing—most of it, anyway. With the bills' serial numbers accounted for, about $4,000 of the Piper ransom showed up in 21 Minnesota communities. But the trail of cash stopped before the law could apprehend the spender. Rumors say the rest of the loot is hidden in Jay Cooke State Park, even though it was delivered to North Minneapolis.

The Piper ransom may be the largest, but it's not the only missing ransom in Minnesota. Missing still is the money given for the return of Edward Bremer, kidnapped in St. Paul in January 1934 by the Barker-Karpis gang for $200,000, one of the largest kidnapping ransoms in the country up to that point. Ma and Fred Barker escaped to Florida with half the ransom. After the FBI there gunned them down, that half was recovered. But legend has it that Ma and Fred buried the other $100,000 in Minnesota along old state Highway 52 beneath a fence post, somewhere between Rochester and Chatfield in Southeastern Minnesota—where (fittingly) residents boast of some of the "richest" farmland in the world. ⚘

Virginia Piper was kidnapped in 1972 from her Orono home.
(photo: Minnesota Historical Society)

Harry Piper spoke with reporters outside of his home in Orono after his wife was abducted.
(photo: Minnesota Historical Society)

UNITED STATES DEPARTMENT OF JUSTICE

FEDERAL BUREAU OF INVESTIGATION

August 8, 1974

KIDNAPING OF MRS. VIRGINIA PIPER, JULY 27, 1972

Mrs. Virginia L. Piper was kidnaped from her Orono, Minnesota, home July 27, 1972. On Friday night, July 28, 1972, a million dollar ransom was delivered to the kidnaper. Mrs. Piper was located by Special Agents of the FBI on July 29, 1972, handcuffed and chained to a tree in the Jay Cook State Park near Duluth, Minnesota.

The individual depicted hereon is an artist's revised sketch of one of the persons believed involved in this kidnaping. This person is described as a white male, in his 40's, 5' 10" tall, stocky build, brown hair combed straight back, brown eyes, wearing metal rimmed glasses, soft spoken, and with a ½" long full face beard.

No person should take any action in this matter which would tend to jeopardize his or her life or safety.

Apprehension and Conviction, Inc., a Minnesota corporation, is offering a $50,000 cash reward for information furnished to the FBI which will lead to the arrest of the persons responsible for Mrs. Piper's kidnaping.

White male, in his 40's, 5'10", stocky build, brown hair combed straight back, brown eyes, metal rimmed glasses, soft spoken, ½" long full face beard.

Joseph H. Trimbach
JOSEPH H. TRIMBACH
Special Agent in Charge
Federal Bureau of Investigation
Minneapolis, Minnesota

The FBI sent out an alert about Virginia Piper's abduction complete with a rendering of a suspect. (graphic: Minnesota Historical Society)

THE RANSOM IS ONE MILLION DOLLARS. THE ENTIRE AMOUNT WILL
BE IN USED UNMARKED TWENTY DOLLAR BILLS. THE MONEY WILL BE
PREPARED IN FOUR SEPARATELY WRAPPED PACKAGES OF TWO HUNDRED
AND FIFTY THOUSAND DOLLARS EACH. THE FOUR PACKAGES WILL BE
DELIVERED IN ONE LARGER CANVAS OR DUCK BAG BROWN OR OLIVE
IN COLOR WITH DRAW STRING TOP. NO ELECTRONIC TRACKING OR
SIGNAL DEVICES WILL BE IN THIS BAG OR THE PACKAGES OF MONEY.
BEFORE THE PRISONER IS SAFELY RETURNED TO YOU THE MONEY WILL
BE EXAMINED FOR OBVIOUS MARKINGS. TESTS WILL BE MADE FOR
UNUSUALLY HIGH MEASURES OF RADIO ACTIVITY AND CONDUCTIVETY
AND THE MONEY WILL BE SUBJECTED TO EXAMINATION WITH INFRA
RED AND ULTRA VIOLET LIGHT. IF THESE OR OTHER DETECTABLE
METHODS OF MARKING ARE FOUND ON ANY PORTION OF THE MONEY IT
WILL NOT BE CONSIDERED ACCEPTIBLE. THE MONEY WILL BE DELIV-
ERED TOMORROW EVENING. THE AMOUNT OF MONEY IS ESTABLISHED
AND WILL NOT BE NEGOTIATED. THE TIME OF DELIVERY HAS BEEN
ESTABLISHED AND WILL NOT BE EXTENDED FOR ANY REASON. THE
PERSON MAKING THE DELIVERY MUST BE CLOSELY ASSOCIATED WITH
THE COMPANY OF P.J.&H. BEFORE DELIVERY IS ACCEPTED THIS PER-
WILL BE EXAMINED FOR AUTHENTICITY. ONLY THE MOST INTIMATE
KNOWLEDGE OF P.J.&H. BUSINESS WILL ENABLE HIM TO SATISFY
THIS EXAMINATION. THE PERSON MAKING THE DELIVERY WILL USE AN
AUTOMOBILE REGISTERED TO HIS HOME ADDRESS. THE MONEY WILL
BE CARRIED IN THE TRUNK OF THE CAR. THE AUTOMOBILE FUEL TANK
MUST BE PREVIOUSELY FILLED BEFORE LEAVING. THE PERSON MAKING
THE DELIVERY WILL CARRY A MINIMUM OF TWO HUNDRED DOLLARS ON
HIS PERSON. HE WILL CARRY AN ASSORTMENT OF CHANGE IN HIS
POCKET INCLUDING AT LEAST FIVE DIMES. HE WILL BE PREPARED TO
LEAVE FROM THE PRISONERS HOME TO MAKE THE DELIVERY AS SOON
AS INSTRUCTIONS ARE RECEIVED AT APPROXIMATELY NINE THIRTY
P.M. WHEN INSTRUCTIONS ARE RECEIVED AT THIS TIME DEPARTURE
WILL BE IMMEDIATE. LAW ENFORCEMENT RADIO FREQUENCIES WILL BE
MONITORED WHILE THE DELIVERY IS IN PROGRESS AND ANY UNUSUALL
ACTIVITY WILL BE NOTED. IF THIS OCCURES THE DELIVERY WILL
NOT BE ACCEPTED. IF THE DELIVERY IS NOT ACCOMPLISHED AS
PLANNED NO FURTHER CONTACT WILL BE MADE. IF ALL INSTRUCTIONS
ARE CAREFULLY FOLLOWED THE SAFETY OF THE PERSON MAKING THE
DELIVERY IS ASSURED. WHEN THE MONEY HAS BEEN RECEIVED IN
ACCORDANCE TO INSTRUCTION THE PRISONER WILL BE SAFELY RELEAS-
ED. THE RELEASE WILL OCCUR AT SIX A.M.

A copy of the ransom note with payment instructions.

Virginia Piper was wearing this sweater when kidnapped and later found in Jay Cooke State Park.

Mrs. Piper was found in Jay Cooke State Park near Duluth two days after her abduction.

Artist's sketches of "persons involved" in the Piper kidnapping, possibly those who spent the marked ransom money. (graphics: Minnesota Historical Society)

Donald Larson and Kenneth Callahan were acquitted of the Piper kidnapping after a retrial. (photo: Minnesota Historical Society)

The front page of the Minneapolis paper after Mrs. Piper's safe return.

The front of Glensheen, the historic Congdon estate, on London Road in Duluth.
(photo: C.J. Boecker) Inset: Chester Congdon, Elisabeth's father, built this mansion and was
the patriarch of the Congdon family. He died in 1916 at 61.

The Congdon Murders
Society Slayings in Duluth

*She believed she was descended from English royalty but she is
amazingly smart—reads a book a day and has a compelling
personality. She was a fabulous cook—had me to dinner at her home
and even baked a birthday cake for the judge during her trial. … She
knit me a wool sweater after she was acquitted.*

–Defense attorney Ron Meshbesher, on Marjorie Congdon
Caldwell, in a 2007 Minnesota Series interview

On rainy nights, the foghorn on Duluth's famed Aerial
Bridge belts out a warning to freighters arriving in the
harbor during shipping season, a definitive sound that can be
heard by most residents. Too bad it can't also sound a warning
for murder. The residents of Glensheen Mansion could have
used it the night of June 26, 1977.

A handful of families founded Duluth and made it
prosper—at the top of this small heap were the Congdons.
Young lawyer Chester Congdon and his wife, Clara, came to
Duluth in 1892, where he became involved in iron ore, lumber,
orchards and the State House of Representatives. His fortune
made, in 1909 Congdon built Glensheen, a 39-room mansion
on prestigious London Road, furnished with items he and
Clara chose after touring castles throughout Europe. Decades
of Duluth schoolchildren attended Congdon Elementary
School and picnicked in Congdon Park. The Congdon name
was respected and known throughout the region.

So it seemed completely unreal when a day nurse arriving for duty at Glensheen on June 27, 1977 discovered that 83-year-old Elisabeth Congdon (daughter of Chester and Clara) had been murdered in her bed, and night nurse Velma Pietila bludgeoned to death.

The murders were horrific—the murderer had broken in a basement window, crept upstairs in the dark and encountered feisty Velma Pietila on the steps. The security system was not turned on and staff heard nothing. Pietila was beaten with a brass candlestick and found on the window seat, her night snack uneaten, her car gone. Elisabeth, even though she had suffered a stroke, was still a strong woman. The medical examiner's report showed she fought hard for her life as she was smothered in her bed by a pillow.

Immediately, Elisabeth's daughter Marjorie and Marjorie's second husband, Roger Caldwell, became prime suspects.

In Roger Caldwell's much later 1983 confession, he described flying to Minneapolis, then taking a bus to Duluth and taking a cab out on London Road. Spotting the mansion, he wandered about and discovered a small, untended cemetery near the house. There he waited, drinking vodka until dark. Making his way to the back of Glensheen, he broke a window in the ground-floor porch. Caldwell stated he crawled in, creeping around the giant pool table in the dark to the stairs. He was not expecting a confrontation, he testified, and the appearance of the night nurse was a surprise. After beating her almost to a pulp in the struggle, he continued on to Elisabeth's bedroom at the top of the stairs, finding her asleep in her bed. Caldwell described, "I took a pillow and put it over her head," he said, telling how he then ransacked drawers looking for valuables. He denied taking a ring off Elisabeth's finger, a ring that was found in Marjorie Caldwell's possession. He also denied that murder was his intention—hard to believe, considering the outcome. Caldwell maintained he was drunk and that burglary was his only motive. He didn't remember driving Pietila's car back to the Minneapolis/St. Paul International Airport, he said.

Caldwell's description of the crime in the transcript of his confession is reproduced in full in Joe Kimball's book, *Secrets of the Congdon Mansion.*

It was the latest in a long line of suspected crimes associated with Caldwell's wife, Marjorie, the Congdon family misfit.

Elisabeth Congdon was the only one of Chester and Clara Congdon's seven children who never married. Longing to be a mother, Elisabeth in the 1930s adopted two baby daughters—Marjorie and Jennifer—unheard of for a single woman at the time. The world Elisabeth created for her daughters at Glensheen was much like her own childhood—privileged, but with a bent toward thriftiness and commitment to community. Hats and white gloves, formal dinners, grand holiday celebrations and charitable giving were hallmarks of the Glensheen lifestyle.

From the beginning, Marjorie had problems fitting in. By her early teens, she had developed alarming tendencies toward rampant spending, lying, jealousies and secrecy—behavior bizarre enough that her mother sent her to the Menninger clinic for an evaluation, where she was diagnosed as sociopathic but left untreated. Prep school letters from Marjorie promised to curb spending while asking for more money. Small fires began to appear near or around her, like in a dressing room fire at a Duluth department store after her charge privileges were revoked at Elisabeth's request.

It was almost a relief to Elisabeth when Marjorie insisted at age 18 on marrying Dick LeRoy. But the out-of-control spending continued. Bills ranged into hundreds of thousands of dollars, and time and time again, Elisabeth and the Congdon trusts bailed her out, according to *Star Tribune*, 1987.

After giving birth to seven children, Marjorie was a devoted but demanding mother, pushing her children into horsemanship and competitive skating, incurring further outrageous spending. Marjorie was not content to simply buy a riding or skating outfit—she would buy it in all sizes or buy up all the bolts of cloth so no one else could have it. She commandeered huge slots of ice time so that others would not be able to practice.

Real estate was another passion; Marjorie bought, sold or lost homes through unstable purchase agreements and bad checks, according to the book *Will to Murder* by former crime reporter Gail Feichtinger, Duluth prosecutor John DeSanto and Duluth investigator Gary Waller. Other times, alarming evidence pointed to evil deeds. Elisabeth had been found very ill the day after Marjorie fed her homemade marmalade during a visit. It was later determined that "Miss Elisabeth" (as she was called by her staff), had a large quantity of muscle relaxant in her system, as described in *Will to Murder*.

After 20 years of bill collectors, fires (including a burned-down garage at their Minneapolis home) and other frustrations, Dick had had enough, and the couple divorced. Marjorie moved to a home in Marine on St. Croix, a house she was later suspected of burning down, according to Glensheen's Daughter: *The Marjorie*

Congdon Story by Sharon Darby Hendry. Marjorie then moved on to Colorado, where she married Roger Caldwell in 1976. Struggling with huge debts, Marjorie and Roger lived in a hotel in Golden, Colo. *Will to Murder* notes that in 1976, fires were set inside a bank that had threatened action against Marjorie's bad checks. Marjorie grew increasingly impatient for the $8 million she would collect from her mother's estate.

On June 24, 1977, three days before the murders, Marjorie wrote out a notarized will promising Roger half of whatever she would inherit from the Congdon estate, a document that police reports show was found in her safe deposit box in Golden State Bank in Golden.

After the murders, evidence led police investigations to quickly document Roger's presence in Duluth on the fateful night. Specific missing jewelry (even Elisabeth's favorite ring wrenched off her finger), a valuable Byzantine coin and a wicker basket all stolen from the murder scene were found in Roger's possession. Twin Cities airport shop personnel remembered him on that day, tying him to a sales receipt. A cab driver remembered driving him from the Duluth airport to London Road near Glensheen. In Golden, Marjorie was out and about that morning, but Roger was not seen. Police reports stated that Marjorie gave several different explanations as to Roger's whereabouts on that morning.

Roger was arrested and indicted on two counts of first-degree murder, Marjorie hiring skilled Minneapolis defense attorney Doug Thomson to defend him. Led by young Duluth prosecutor John De Santo, the trial began in April 1978 in Brainerd. Though certain questions were left unanswered and there was evidence of shoddy police work during the initial investigation, Roger was found guilty and sentenced to two life terms at Stillwater State Prison. The most damning piece of evidence was a fingerprint on an envelope containing the collectible coin stolen during the murder and mailed from Duluth to Roger in Colorado.

One month after the verdict, Marjorie was indicted on four counts of aiding and conspiracy to commit murder in the first degree. Held in Hastings, Marjorie's trial was different. Criminal attorney Ron Meshbesher presented a brilliant defense, demolishing the prosecution's case. Meshbesher raised doubts, including discrediting the damning fingerprint, resulting in Marjorie's full acquittal.

By this time, Marjorie was off with a new man. Wally Hagen and his wife, Helen, had been buddies with Marjorie during the skating years. As skating families, they were almost inseparable, but later Helen developed Alzheimer's disease and was confined to a nursing home. In 1980, after a visit from Marjorie, according to the *Tucson Weekly*, a nurse saw her hand-feeding Helen baby food from a jar; Helen Hagen fell into a coma and died. In August 1981, Marjorie married Wally Hagen, 20 years her senior, committing bigamy in North Dakota by not having first divorced Roger Caldwell.

Roger was granted a new trial in 1982 and released from prison after serving just five years, based on questions raised during Marjorie's trial and subsequent acquittal. Rather than re-try the case, Duluth prosecutors struck a deal with Roger Caldwell in 1983 to confess, limiting his incarceration to time served. Roger's rambling confession never explained some of the unknown details about the murders and never implicated Marjorie.

Having recanted his confession, and battling alcoholism, Roger Caldwell committed suicide in 1988. *Minneapolis Star Tribune* writer Joe Kimball, the reporter on the case, interviewed Roger after his release and found him a sad figure. "I think in his heart he always believed Marjorie would swoop in and save him somehow but she never did," said Kimball in a 2007 interview.

Marjorie and new husband Wally settled into a historic property, Cranberry House in Mound, Minn., selling it just a year later. Before the new owners could take possession, however, the house burned to the ground. This time, the evidence against Marjorie was solid. Notwithstanding Ron Meshbesher's defense, Marjorie was convicted of arson in February 1984 and subsequently served 20 months at the women's prison in Shakopee. (According to Meshbesher, there are sides of Marjorie that few understood. "She was very well-liked in prison and re-organized the entire cafeteria service while she was incarcerated in Minnesota," he said.)

After her release, she and Wally moved to Ajo, Ariz., where her grandfather had owned land and had mining interests years before. A series of suspicious fires begin to appear in the area, according to newspaper reports. Marjorie was caught again committing arson, convicted and was to begin a 15-year prison sentence in 1992. Somehow she convinced the judge to give her 24 hours to make arrangements for Wally, who she always said had multiple illnesses, including cancer. During that 24-hour period, Wally was found dead of a drug overdose plus a little suspected help from a tampered gas line, according to a

Star Tribune story. Again, Marjorie was arrested and charged with murder, but the charge didn't stick for lack of hard evidence. In October 1992, Marjorie began her 15-year sentence at the state prison in Tucson. An autopsy revealed no cancer in Wally's body, according to *Will to Murder*.

After 12 years, Marjorie earned early release from prison in 2004. Her children are estranged from her, having fought battles objecting to her parole and after an extended court case to keep Marjorie from controlling her inherited Congdon trusts. Marjorie also fought in court with Wally's estranged children over his ashes; a judge finally divided them in half as a settlement. Her youngest son, Rick, became interested in law and went to work for the Legal Rights Center in Minneapolis.

But the story was not over. In 2007, 30 years after the murders at Glensheen (and even while tourists daily toured the mansion, now owned by the University of Minnesota)—Marjorie was arrested again. After forming a friendship with Roger Sammis, an elderly man in a Tucson nursing home, Marjorie gained his Power of Attorney just before he mysteriously died. Marjorie, with her legal power, had him cremated before his family knew he was dead. A few days later, she tried to endorse and transfer a large check of his to her personal account. At the time of this writing, 75-year-old Marjorie Congdon LeRoy Caldwell Hagen is awaiting trial for fraud, forgery, theft and computer tampering. The death itself cannot be investigated because there is no body.

Elisabeth Congdon, Velma Pietila, Helen Hagen, Wally Hagen and Roger Sammis are all dead. Roger Caldwell died in disgrace by his own hand. Is it over? Stay tuned.

Duluth woman, nurse slain

By Peg Meier and Joe Kimball
Staff Writers

Elisabeth Congdon, 83 years old and one of Minnesota's richest people, was found slain in a bed of her Duluth mansion early Monday morning, a pillow smothering her face.

Her nurse, Velma Pietila, also was killed in the 39-room house. She had been beaten over the head with an 8-inch brass candlestick and died in a pool of blood on a stairway landing.

Elisabeth Congdon

Duluth police said last night they had no suspects in the case, which has all the elements of the opening chapters in an Agatha Christie mystery.

Inspector Ernie Grams said the motive apparently was robbery. "An empty jewelry box was on the floor of the bedroom and the room was ransacked," he said.

A car stolen from the estate was found yesterday at the Minneapolis-St. Paul International Airport. Authorities were concentrating their investigation on the North Shore of Lake Superior and at the airport during the day yesterday. But by evening they admitted they were back to combing the house and car for clues.

The bodies of the two women were found at 7 a.m. yesterday by a nurse who was to relieve Mrs. Pietila of nursing duties. Miss Congdon had suffered a stroke about 8 years ago and had around-the-clock nursing help. Paralyzed on one side, she was confined to a wheelchair.

A chauffeur and a gardener live on the 7½-acre estate but sleep in servants' quarters in separate buildings, police said. A cook was in the mansion Sunday night; she slept in a different wing from Miss Congdon and Mrs. Pietila. The cook, Prudence Renquist, said she heard no unusual noises during the night. She told police, however, that her poodle started barking at about 3 a.m.

A 7-foot-high fence made of brick and metal surrounds the estate. Two gates were kept padlocked.

Police theorized that the assailant or assailants broke into the house through a rear window in the basement, which they found broken. Mrs. Pietila apparently heard noises and went to investigate. Her bedroom was across the hall from Miss Congdon's. She was hit at least once, and very hard, with the candlestick, police said, and fell down six steps to a landing. She climbed onto or was placed on a windowseat on the landing, where she was found.

Blood, apparently Mrs. Pietila's, was found on Miss Congdon's pillow. Police said blood apparently had gotten on the killer, who had then rubbed against the pillow.

Mrs. Pietila had been a regular nurse for Miss Congdon until May, when she retired at age 65. Her husband said she was asked to work Sunday night to fill in for a nurse who wanted the night off.

Loren Pietila, her husband, was notified of the slayings and got to the mansion about 8 a.m. He discovered that his wife's car, a 1976 white and tan Ford Granada, was missing. Later in the morning police from the Minneapolis-St. Paul International Airport called

Congdon continued on page 4A

Staff Photo by Darlene Pfister

A Duluth policeman guarded the entrance of the Congdon mansion Monday

Elisabeth Congdon (top left) and her nurse, Velma Pietila, were victims of the attacks. Newspapers statewide announced the Congdon murders. (photos: AP, Minnesota Historical Society and *Star Tribune*)

Top: Roger Caldwell is said to have entered the Congdon estate from the adjacent cemetery on London Road. Bottom: The majestic back view of Glensheen Mansion. (photo: C.J. Boecker)

Top: The balcony at the back of the Congdon estate and the ground-floor porch, also known as the subway.

The pool room and staircase inside the Congdon estate.
(photos: courtesy UMD/Glensheen)

Roger Caldwell is escorted to court in Brainerd in 1978. (photo: AP)

Marjorie Congdon Caldwell awaits trial with her son Ricky LeRoy in Dakota County in 1979.
(photo: AP)

Top: John DeSanto prosecuted both Marjorie Congdon Caldwell and Roger Caldwell and co-wrote the book *Will To Murder*. Marjorie Congdon Caldwell leaves the Duluth courthouse during her court proceedings with her attorney, Ron Meshbesher, and son Ricky LeRoy.

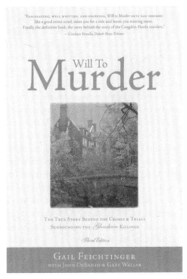

Clockwise from upper left: Marjorie Congdon Hagen in a 2007 photo in Arizona. (photo: KARE 11). The movie *You'll Like My Mother* was filmed at the Congdon estate five years prior to the murders. *Will to Murder*, the definitive book on the case, was co-authored by prosecutor John DeSanto. *Star Tribune* reporter Joe Kimball wrote *Secrets of The Congdon Mansion*. Kimball was one of the few to attend Roger Caldwell's funeral.

Brad Dunlap and Anne Barber Dunlap shown in photos near the time of her murder, and the Dunlaps at their wedding. (photos: Minnesota Historical Society and the Barber family)

The Case of Anne Barber Dunlap
One of the Twin Cities' Highest-Profile Murders Still a Mystery

On Saturday, Dec. 30, 1995, 31-year-old Anne Barber Dunlap was leading her typically active life filled with family, friends and activities. In the morning, she completed a 10-mile run with her running club, the Fireball Fuchsias, before they stopped and had brunch together. Back at home, at 2:30 p.m. she set out again, telling her husband, Brad, she was going to the Mall of America to buy a pair of shoes. She left the South Minneapolis home and drove her 1987 maroon Toyota Celica to the mall, where, it was later learned, sales clerks at Nordstrom's and Macy's remember talking with her. She planned to meet Brad back at the house in early evening to go out for dinner.

She never returned.

At 8 that night, Brad called Anne's parents, Donn and Louise Barber, who were at their cabin near Annandale, and alerted them that Anne was missing. The Barbers headed back to their home near Lake Calhoun—the same house where Brad reported last seeing his wife that afternoon, since they had been temporarily living there with Anne's parents while the younger couple built their "dream home" on seven acres in Medina. That night all three spread out in search of Anne and her car—driving the route they imagined Anne would've taken to the Mall of America, combing the Southdale mall parking lot, driving to the Medina house, and calling hospitals, Mall of

America security, Minneapolis police, Bloomington police and the State Patrol.

At 7:40 a.m. Dec. 31, Brad Dunlap filed a missing-person report with the Minneapolis police.

Quickly, groups of family and friends were organized in a metro-wide search, distributing posters and notifying the media of her disappearance. On New Year's Day 1996, about 8 a.m., one such group found Anne Dunlap's car at the Kmart at 10 W. Lake St. in Minneapolis, the keys in the unlocked car. They ran to enlist the help of police officers they had seen at a nearby Perkins. Television crews were on hand to record the unfolding events by the time police returned with bloodhounds. Anne's car was towed to the police forensic garage, where the trunk was opened. Inside was the body of Anne Barber Dunlap, whom authorities later said died of sharp force injuries to her head and neck, repeatedly stabbed in the throat and neck. Her diamond ring was missing.

The case immediately became, and remains today, one of the highest-profile murders in Twin Cities history. The police wasted no time in focusing on Brad Dunlap as the prime suspect, and he has remained so through the years. But unwaveringly, from the beginning, the Barbers have stood steadfast in their public support of Brad Dunlap and belief in his innocence. As of this writing, the case is still unsolved.

According to a *Star Tribune* timeline, at around 4 p.m. on New Year's Day 1996, homicide investigators questioned Brad Dunlap for about five hours. He returned home that night and told the Barbers that police suspect him as the killer. In a *Star Tribune* report later that month, the Barbers said that when he walked into their house that night after being interviewed by police for five hours—he collapsed into uncontrollable sobbing. When he finally spoke after 20 minutes, he said, "She's dead, and they say I did it," Louise Barber recalled.

That night, police arrived to search the Barber (and temporary Dunlap) home for the first time. On Jan. 4, they returned for another search. "It's routine follow-up. It was the last place where we know she was at for sure," said Minneapolis police Lt. Mark Ellenberg told a *Star Tribune* reporter.

After all these years, the Barbers stand by Brad. In a 2008 Minnesota Series interview, Donn Barber said of that night: "Brad was more upset than any of us. He cried and cried nonstop."

From the start, media attention was intense, with reporters camping outside the Barbers' home, and daily coverage and speculation in and out of the press. This was not a typical city homicide. It was a story that shook the security of the Minnesota middle class: a 31-year-old professional white woman slain on a suburban shopping trip. If it could happen to Anne, it could surely happen to anyone, and the public wanted answers.

On Jan. 6, the women in Anne Barber Dunlap's running club wept and held one another before leading 237 runners on the same Minneapolis route Dunlap and the group had run seven days before. Saturday's memorial run in Dunlap's honor was renamed "the Dunlap 10-Miler," and the group changed to "Forever Fuchsia," also in her honor. The runners, many from Northwest clubs in the metro area, ran with fuchsia ribbons on their jackets and posters on their backs offering a $75,000 reward for the capture of Dunlap's killer.

Throughout the preceding the week, Brad Dunlap
had been the primary focus of the police investigation.
But Dunlap said his wife had no reason to "disappear" because
they were living a great life—earning good money (she as
marketing manager at Pillsbury, responsible for the Hungry
Jack line of refrigerated dough products; he as sales manager
at Environmental Graphics in Hopkins); building their dream
home (which would require both of their paychecks); and
planning to have children. But even while unrelenting press
reports and public opinion talked of Brad as suspect, Donn and
Louise Barber stood resolutely convinced of his innocence.

During a three-hour interview the Barbers talked
about their affection for Dunlap and their unwavering belief
that he was not capable of harming their daughter, according
to a Jan. 14, 1996 *Star Tribune* report. Their lawyer, Bill Mauzy,
said they agreed to the interview to let the public know that
they know Brad like a son and they know he is not the killer.
They reminisced about the good times they had—spending
nearly every weekend with Brad and Anne at their cabin,
celebrating Brad's birthday on a beach in Mexico, and for the
prior two months, living in the same home.

The Barbers told *Star Tribune* reporters that Anne and
Brad had a deep affection for each other that was "remarkable
and unshakable." And on Christmas night, Louise Barber
marveled at their affection, she said, after she caught a glimpse
of the two—who had been married eight years—standing in a
hall of her brother's home, kissing.

Still, police attention toward and public speculation
of Brad skyrocketed when it was learned that just five

months before the murder, Anne's life insurance had been upgraded from $100,000 to $1 million, and that Brad was the beneficiary. But that was at the advice of a financial planner they visited at Anne Dunlap's suggestion, said her parents at the time, and Brad's policy had also been upgraded (from $500,000 to $1 million).

By Jan. 26, the Barbers had withdrawn most of the reward money offered for information leading to the arrest and charging of a suspect. Donn and Louise Barber withdrew $65,000 of the $75,000 reward because they were concerned it might lead "to false information which might hinder rather than further the criminal investigation," according to a news release.

The $65,000 represented money offered by the Barbers, friends and companies associated with the Barbers, the press release said. The remaining $10,000 was a contribution made by Anne Dunlap's employer, Pillsbury, which remained in effect.

Time passed, and there were no new leads. In June that year, runners gathered again—1,200 strong this time, in the midst of fuchsia balloons and the presence of Donn and Louise Barber and Brad Dunlap, who all stood at the finish line handing out fuchsia carnations in the first Anne Barber Dunlap Memorial 5K and 10K race.

In October that year, Brad Dunlap filed a suit in an attempt to collect the $1 million in life insurance. In May 1997, he filed documents in federal court claiming that the Minneapolis Police Department and Anne Barber Dunlap's insurance company were working in unison to avoid paying him the insurance benefits. He asked that all documents that the police department gave to the Chubb Life Insurance Co. of America be given to him so that the matter could be heard in federal court.

"Chubb has enlisted the help of the Minneapolis Police Department to support an allegation that Bradley Dunlap killed his wife," said a memorandum filed in federal court in Minneapolis. The allegation is being used, in part, so that Chubb can avoid paying more than $1 million in death benefits, it said.

Chubb Life Insurance refused to pay, citing a police affidavit that says the lead investigator believes Dunlap killed his wife. Chubb alleges the policy is invalid because Dunlap was planning to kill his wife when he completed the application Aug. 18, 1995.

By July 1997, Brad Dunlap, still the prime suspect in the slaying of his wife, quit his job and moved to the Southwest to gain privacy.

In late September that year, as reported in the *Star Tribune*, a judge ruled that Minneapolis police must turn over investigative documents to the attorneys of Brad Dunlap, who was seeking videotapes of witness interviews, interview summaries, his interview with police and results of forensic tests.

In October 1998, Brad Dunlap, the insurance company and Donn Barber (acting as the personal representative of his daughter's estate) reached an out-of-court settlement in the life insurance benefits. The details of the settlement were not disclosed. Anne Dunlap was also believed to have a $745,000 policy through her job at Pillsbury, but Pillsbury did not reveal whether Brad Dunlap received those benefits.

Brad Dunlap is living a new life in Arizona, reportedly remarried, and Donn and Louise Barber have continued to supported him, convinced he would not have harmed their daughter. They keep in touch, visiting yearly, Donn Barber said in a 2008 interview.

The case remains in public consciousness, still unsolved. In 2005, WCCO crime reporter Caroline Lowe blogged about the crime on its 10th anniversary:

"People still can't forget the images from this crime. They remember the news videotape of police inspecting her abandoned car in a Kmart parking lot as her husband waited nearby. People ask me if he is still a suspect and wonder if her parents are still convinced of his innocence. ... Eventually, the news coverage subsided, and Brad Dunlap left Minneapolis to build a new life, out of the glare of the media spotlight."

Anne's brother, Paul, still maintains a website, in the event anyone has new information that could lead to the apprehension of her killer: www.paulbarber.net/annemiss. html. And anyone with information helpful to the investigation can call the Minneapolis Police Department's Homicide Unit at (612) 673-2941.

Do the Barbers have any theory of their own regarding who murdered their daughter? "I have no idea, none," responded Donn Barber in 2008 as this book was going to press. "Unless some crook in prison talks sometime. Or one of their girlfriends gets mad and talks. We don't hear from the police. It's a cold case." ☷☷

Anne Barber Dunlap was last seen at the Mall of America, where she was shopping for shoes, on Dec. 30, 1995. Donn and Louise Barber, Anne's parents pictured during the case.

At the time of Anne's disappearance, the Dunlaps lived in the upscale Lake Calhoun area, with Anne's parents, while their new house was being built.

Anne Dunlap's body was found in the trunk of her red Toyota Celica in the Kmart parking lot at Nicollet and Lake in Minneapolis.

Brad Dunlap pictured in Arizona, years after his wife's death. One week after Anne's disappearance, the Barbers and Brad Dunlap looked on as Anne's running club traced the course she ran on the day of her disappearance. A race was named in Anne's honor.
(photos: Minnesota Historical Society and the Barber family)

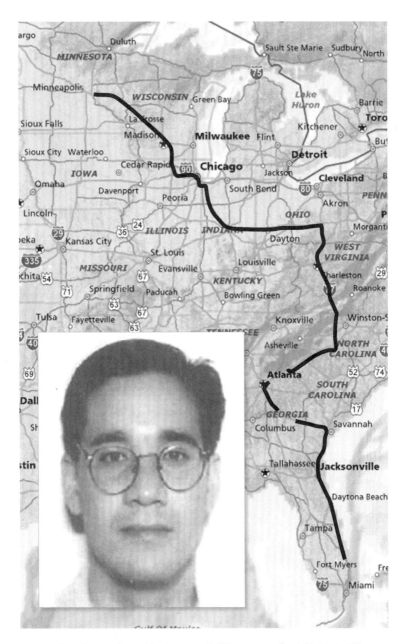

Andrew Cunanan began his crime spree in Minnesota, ending in Florida in 1997.

Serial Killer Andrew Cunanan
Minneapolis Murder Starts Nationwide Manhunt

David Madson was missing. Friends and co-workers became alarmed when Madson, 33, an architect and dedicated worker, missed an important meeting at Minneapolis' John Ryan Co., his employer, on Monday, April 28, 1997, and didn't show up on Tuesday either. Phone calls went unanswered. Knowing this was unlike him, friends asked the caretaker at his apartment building in the Minneapolis Warehouse District for help.

When the building caretaker and another resident entered the apartment at Harmony Lofts on Tuesday, they smelled and saw the body of a man rolled up in an Oriental rug. At first, police thought the body was Madson's, but it proved to be that of Jeffrey Trail. Madson was gone, along with his Grand Jeep Cherokee, reported the *Star Tribune*.

Friends had seen Madson on both Friday and Saturday nights with someone from California named Andrew Cunanan, who was staying with him. Quickly tracing movements over the previous several days in Minneapolis and California, police learned that Cunanan had told friends he was going to Minneapolis to reconnect with his true love, David Madson. Police investigations showed that Cunanan also knew and socialized with Jeffrey Trail, whom he had most likely met in San Diego, while Trail was in the Navy. Trail, a graduate of the U.S. Naval Academy at Annapolis, was described as a top student. Cunanan told friends he had some business to settle with

Jeffrey, noted the *Star Tribune*. All three men were known to be homosexual and living a gay lifestyle although both Minneapolis men's families were unaware of their sexual orientation.

On Sunday, April 27, a message from Cunanan on Trail's answering machine invited him to Madson's apartment. Police reports show that Trail was bludgeoned to death on that Sunday night. The weapon was presumed to be a claw hammer found at the scene. Trail's watch was stopped at 9:55 p.m.

Who was the murderer? Cunanan? Madson? Both? Speculation was rampant. Strangely, witnesses told police they saw Madson and a man believed to be Cunanan walking Madson's dog both Monday and Tuesday mornings, after the murder. Early police thinking centered on Madson as the killer, but both Madson and Cunanan had disappeared. Later, investigators "found nothing to indicate that Madson was involved in Trail's death and there is evidence that Andrew Cunanan was," Minneapolis police Captain Steve Strehlow told *Star Tribune*.

Madson was well-connected and charming, according to the *Star Tribune*, having graduated from the University of Minnesota, Duluth, then earning a master's degree at the University's Twin Cities campus. He had a wide circle of friends in both the gay and straight communities. He had lectured at Harvard. The police learned that Madson was said to have been intimate with Cunanan in the past, but that he had distanced himself from the relationship, reported the *Star Tribune*. At John Ryan, he designed kiosks and installations for banks nationwide. David's family, frantic at his disappearance, was also deeply disturbed by the initial police suggestion that David had committed Trail's murder, something they felt he could never do.

Inquiries in California revealed that Jeffrey Trail had met Andrew Cunanan at various clubs in San Diego and hung around with him for a while, but, after a stint with the California Highway Patrol following his discharge from the Navy, had recently moved to Bloomington, Minn., for a job as district manager for Ferrellgas, a national supplier of propane gas. Cunanan was known to have visited both men in the Twin Cities on several occasions.

The saga unfolded rapidly. On Saturday of the same week, David Madson's body was found by two fishermen in a remote spot along the shore of East Rush Lake in Chisago County, an hour north of the Twin Cities. He had been shot in the head and back. According to the *Star Tribune*, there was one possible sighting on Friday, May 2, when a motorist said he saw two men in what he believed to be Madson's Jeep Cherokee. The Jeep was driving erratically near the Rush City exit, said the motorist. Madson may have been killed that same day, thought police, shot with a 40-caliber gun (the same type of gun that was known to belong to Jeffrey Trail).

Now two sets of police investigations in both Minneapolis and Chisago County were under way; but by nightfall on Saturday, the Jeep Cherokee was parked on a street in Chicago's Gold Coast neighborhood.

On Sunday, May 4, wealthy cosmetics queen Marilyn Miglin—a Home Shopping Network regular for her personal line of cosmetics—arrived at her elegant townhouse in Chicago wondering why her husband, 72-year-old real estate magnate Lee Miglin, had failed to pick her up at the airport. She knew something was wrong the moment she stepped inside. The house was in disarray—wet towels, food and dishes around, evidence of shaving stubble not her husband's—a situation her fastidious husband would never have tolerated. Frightened, she enlisted help from neighbors. They discovered Lee dead in the garage, bound and gagged, his throat slashed. (Police files indicated that Miglin was dead by noon on Saturday, just one day after Madson was killed.) Police believe Madson's Jeep Cherokee had been seen parked in Chicago Saturday. Now Miglin's dark-green Lexus was missing. All signs pointed to Andrew Cunanan.

The search for Cunanan went national. Now the Chicago police had a full investigation going, as did the two jurisdictions in Minnesota. National media reported that May 4 cellular phone signals from the Lexus were monitored in Philadelphia and western Pennsylvania. Police began to track Cunanan's movements through this mechanism, which was evidently triggered whenever the car was in gear. Cunanan must have seen these news reports because the car, found later, showed that he had tried to disengage the phone. But where was Cunanan—and who was he?

Andrew Cunanan, 27, was the youngest child of a Filipino father and Sicilian mother, Modesto (Pete) and MaryAnn Cunanan. In San Diego, he grew up in an unhappy and financially troubled household but was doted on by his mentally fragile mother. His father deserted the family and went back to the Philippines when Andrew was in his teens. According to published reports, early on he began embellishing his life to friends. His mother sent Andrew to an exclusive prep school where he made contact with students from wealthy families, reported the *Star Tribune*. Cunanan appeared to tell friends he had a wealthy family background. Maureen Orth, in her 1999 book *Vulgar Favors*, tells a mesmerizing story of Cunanan's manipulative life and entry into gay society in California. Orth's well-researched book weaves endless tales of selling rough sex and drugs to achieve money and position. Cunanan was entranced by the lives of the rich and famous, and maneuvered himself into that milieu—trading, dealing, prostituting—whatever it took to maintain a high-living lifestyle for himself. Drugs, wild sex games, gay bars, spas, discos and constantly changing partners were rife in the gay communities where Cunanan hung out.

Among other relationships, the *Star Tribune* named Norman Blachford, a rich San Diego industrialist, who had recently supported Cunanan, taking him to Cap Ferrat, France and giving him an expensive car. Blachford was a meal ticket for Cunanan, but Cunanan left him for younger men. According to Orth, Cunanan both dealt and used drugs such as crystal meth, aka "speed," which can cause erratic, violent behavior.

After Blachford, Cunanan's subsequent meeting with David Madson changed his romantic life but not his habits. Perhaps strung out on drugs, he saw Madson as his great love and possibly Jeffrey Trail as a spoiler of that opportunity. No one knows for sure what kicked off this killing spree, but it wasn't over yet.

While Cunanan's relationships to Trail and Madson were known, the Miglin murder seemed inexplicable. Was it simply random? Police didn't think so, and there was a concerted effort to find a possible homosexual connection between Cunanan and Lee or his son Duke, an actor living in California. Cunanan had sometimes said he had connections to a real estate developer named Duke in Chicago, says Orth in *Vulgar Favors*. The family's prominence shut down these investigations and a connection was never proven.

Now it seemed that Andrew Cunanan had committed three murders: Jeffrey Trail, David Madson and Lee Miglin. But it didn't stop there.

On Friday, May 9, cemetery caretaker William Reese, 45, was shot in the head with a 40-caliber gun in an obscure Civil War burial ground in southern New Jersey. Miglin's Lexus was abandoned at the scene and the caretaker's red pickup truck was missing. Police surmised that this one was, indeed, a random killing because Cunanan needed to switch cars. Part of the chase, according to the *Star Tribune*, involved a license plate taken on May 10 from a car parked in Florence County, S.C.

The FBI had been called into the case by this time, and after the Reese murder, Cunanan was added to the FBI's Ten Most Wanted List. Andrew Cunanan, the boy "who always wanted to be someone," said his father in newspaper reports, was front-page news, on television and magazine covers throughout the country. The FBI spokesperson on the case was Coleen Rowley in the Minneapolis office (who later became an FBI whistleblower over the buildup to 9/11). "I can't imagine how we could put any more resources into the case," she told *Star Tribune* at the time. "We have the FBI and a national fugitive task force working on it and local and state authorities following up on tips."

Then, nothing. After two weeks of near hysteria, the trail grew cold. In reality, Cunanan had taken himself to Miami near South Beach, renting a room at the slightly seedy Normandy Plaza Hotel, with the red truck parked in plain sight on Collins Avenue. His cross-cultural looks allowing him to blend in, he lived here quietly for several weeks. He used his own name and hotel address as he pawned a coin (proved to be from Lee Miglin's collection), then moved the truck to a nearby public garage, police reports later showed.

Cunanan sold drugs and prostituted for money in Miami Beach, but overall, laid low. His favorite magazines were reputed to be *Vogue, Vanity Fair* and *Architectural Digest,* all of which detailed the life he craved, according to *Vulgar Favors.* At the top of his celebrity-studded world was sometime Miami resident and famous designer Gianni Versace, whom Cunanan claimed to have met and spent time with in 1990 in San Francisco. (However, the Versace family never admitted that Gianni Versace and Andrew Cunanan had ever met.)

On Tuesday, July 15, still using Jeffrey Trail's 40-caliber gun that he used in the Madson, Miglin and Reese murders, Andrew Cunanan shot down famed designer Gianni Versace on the steps of his Miami Beach mansion. He walked calmly away in front of an eyewitness, slipping through police cordons that were placed immediately after emergency calls were received. Various witnesses followed Cunanan's movements immediately after the murder, telling police they saw him entering a nearby public parking ramp. Checking the ramp, police found the pickup truck where Cunanan had parked it some weeks earlier bearing the missing South

Carolina license plate, reported the *Star Tribune*. Evidence showed Cunanan had changed clothes in the truck and then presumably fled on foot.

Eight days later, a Miami houseboat caretaker suspected someone was hiding on the houseboat he cared for belonging to a millionaire. A police, helicopter and media frenzy, reminiscent of the recent O.J. Simpson Ford Bronco chase, quickly surrounded the boat. When police finally entered some hours later, Andrew Cunanan was dead of a self-inflicted gunshot through the mouth, the 40-caliber and a *Vogue* magazine nearby.

How could this spree killer have eluded capture for almost three months, even though hundreds of FBI agents and police throughout the country were alerted to his movements? How could he have hidden in plain sight on Miami Beach for two months, with Reese's truck (which was on every national watch list) overlooked? The search was marked by investigative bumbling, lack of jurisdictional cooperation and missed opportunities, according to a *Star Tribune* interview with Orth. "There was a prosecutors' view that they had to have an airtight case," said Orth. "And police were constrained by the need to follow a certain procedure…with Andrew Cunanan, this allowed him to go free and race out of sight," she said.

The Gianni Versace murder and Cunanan's death ends this story. Celebrities by the hundreds, including Princess Diana and Elton John, attended Versace's funeral in Milan, Italy. Ironically, just six weeks later, Princess Diana herself was dead. And Andrew Cunanan had achieved international notoriety and the recognition he once desperately craved. ⚡

Chapter 7

Andrew Cunanan stayed in the downtown warehouse district during his time in Minneapolis.

Clockwise from top left: Andrew Cunanan's wanted poster, Jeffrey Trail, David Madson and Lee Miglin. Trail, Madson and Miglin were the first three of Cunanan's victims.

Andrew Cunanan's path in 1997 included the downtown Minneapolis club scene and Rush City, Minn. (photo: Susan K. Timothy)

Designer Gianni Versace was Cunanan's fifth victim, killed on the steps of
his Miami Beach mansion. (photo: Cindy D. David)

As television helicopters hovered overhead, Andrew Cunanan was found dead in this Miami Beach houseboat at the conclusion of a nationwide manhunt in 1997. (photo: AP)

Famous Defense Attorneys of Minnesota

Doug Thomson, the son of a railroad manager, graduated from William Mitchell College of Law and practiced from his St. Paul office for decades. Famous as a stern litigator and vicious cross examiner, Thomson was also known as a fastidious dresser and for his practical jokes. Famous defendants included Norman Mastrian (in the Carol Thompson case), Connie Trimble (for her role in the murder of St. Paul police officer James Sackett), and Roger Caldwell (in the murder of Elisabeth Congdon). Outside the courtroom, Thomson was known for his soft-spoken, thoughtful nature. He passed away in Roseville in 2007.

Ronald Meshbesher was born in Minneapolis and graduated from the University of Minnesota. Known for litigation and handling evidence, he wrote *The Trial Handbook for Minnesota Lawyers*. Meshbesher has tried famous cases involving Piper kidnapping defendants Kenneth Callahan and Donald Larson; defendants in the Eunice Kronholm kidnapping; the Congdon murder trial; and others. A sought-after legal expert, Meshbesher currently practices with his firm, Meshbesher and Spence in Minneapolis.

Joe Friedberg was born in New York City and graduated from the University of North Carolina Law School. After moving to Minnesota, he became a renowned and passionate courtroom litigator defending famous murder cases involving June Mikulanec in 1978, Gary Splett in 1982, Harold Jurgens, and Russell Lund in the early-'90s. Friedberg, an avid horseman, is known for occasionally wearing cowboy boots with his suits.

Earl Gray attended Gustavus Adolphus and The William Mitchell College of Law, beginning his practice in 1970. Gray became famous for defending Robert Bentz in the Jordan, Minn., child abuse case of the 1980s. Gray has handled cases from murder to misdemeanors. A vigorous defender of high-profile clients, Gray has tried U.S., Wisconsin and Minnesota cases involving celebrities and athletes in a variety of charges.

J. Anthony Torres, a graduate of William Mitchell College of Law, came to the forefront of Minnesota defense attorneys in 1992 with his defense of Robert Guevara in the case of Corrine Erstad's disappearance in Inver Grove Heights. Torres, an astute researcher and high-profile litigator, has gone on to try numerous cases.

Top Cops

Mayors from Duluth, Minneapolis and St. Paul all had law enforcement connections. Herb Bergson of Duluth was a detective and mayor in Superior, Wis. Charles Stenvig was a Minneapolis police officer before serving two terms as mayor in the '70s.

Charlie McCarty of St. Paul, pictured here leading the St. Paul City Council in the '70s (which included council members Vic Tedesco, Rosalie Butler and Len Levine), patrolled the city in his Lincoln.

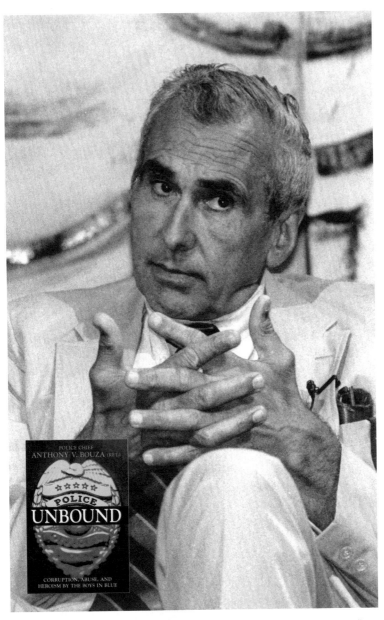

Tony Bouza was born in Spain and moved from the NYPD to serve as Minneapolis police chief from 1980-'89. Bouza, who ran for governor of Minnesota in 1994, is author of books including *Police Unbound*. (photos: courtesy Prometheus Books)

Top Cops

Coleen Rowley, a former FBI agent and chief legal adviser in the Minneapolis FBI office beginning in 1990, gained fame as a whistleblower when she testified in front of the Senate and the 9/11 Commission about the FBI's internal mishandling of information related to the Sept. 11, 2001 terrorist attacks. Rowley was named *TIME* "Person of the Year" in 2002 along with two other whistleblowers. She retired from the FBI in 2004 after 24 years with the agency. In 2006, Rowley ran for the U.S. Congress but lost to John Kline.

Clockwise from top left: James Sackett, Bob Fletcher, Rich Stanek and Don Omodt. James Sackett was killed answering a call in St. Paul in May 1970. Bob Fletcher has served as Ramsey County sheriff, police officer, council member and ran for mayor of St. Paul. Hennepin County Sheriff Rich Stanek took a prominent role in the 35W Bridge collapse and served multiple terms in the Minnesota Legislature. Don Omodt was a longtime Hennepin County sheriff.

Minneapolis Trucker's Strike of 1934

In 1934, the Teamsters struck against most of the trucking companies in Minneapolis. The strike paved the way for the organization of over-the-road drivers and the growth of the Teamsters union. This strike, sometimes called a police riot, was one of the most violent in the state's history, and a major battle in Minnesota's "civil war" of the 1930s between business and labor.

A non-union city, Minneapolis business leaders had successfully kept unions at bay through an organization called the Citizens Alliance, but by 1934, unions were gaining strength. By early May 1934, General Drivers Local 574 of the International Brotherhood of Teamsters had organized 3,000 truckers into a union. When employers refused to recognize the union, union leaders called a strike. Trucking operations in the city came to a halt.

The strike began on May 16, 1934, shutting down most commercial transport in the city. Police and National Guard were called in to guard trucks, and the Citizens Alliance activated the local militia. Conflict escalated daily throughout May and reached a peak late in the month, at the city market, where strikers clashed with police, who were trying to open it for farm produce to be brought in. Many women strike supporters joined the strikers and were severely beaten. Hundreds of strikers were arrested. In support of the truckers, 35,000 building trades workers went on strike. The battle raged on violently for two days. The strike ended on May 25, when the union was recognized and their demands settled. By that time, there were 200 injured and four dead from the conflict. ☙

–sources: Minnesota Historical Society, Wikipedia

Teamsters and police in Minneapolis clashed in 1934 during the Trucker's Strike.
(photos: Minnesota Historical Society)

Journalism Behind Bars

After he and his two brothers had served nearly 10 years in Stillwater prison for the botched robbery of the Northfield bank with the Jesse James gang in 1876, Cole Younger led the efforts to launch the prison's first newspaper. *The Prison Mirror* was an immediate success upon its debut on Aug. 10, 1887. Merchants bought ads. Copies were sold by newsboys in Stillwater for a nickel. Subscriptions for $1 poured in from around the country.

It is now the country's longest-running, continuously published prison newspaper. *The Prison Mirror* has been covered by the *New York Times* and *Time* magazine, and won awards including the American Penal Press Contest in 1985 and 1986 as the nation's best prison newspaper.

The startup plan was for the newspaper to be funded and created solely by inmates. Among the top contributers to the paper's original "trust fund," according to the book *Jailhouse Journalism: The Fourth Estate Behind Bars* by James McGrath Morris, were Cole and James Younger ($20 each) and Robert Younger ($10). For prisoners earning 30 to 45 cents a day, these were major contributions.

The newspaper is rarely censored. In 1989, Warden Robert Erickson told *Time* the newspaper has a fourth-estate status he would not like to challenge: "Cole Younger would turn over in his grave, with his six-shooters blazing," he said. ⚖

Cole, Jim and Bob Younger. (photos: Minnesota Historical Society)

The Early Years

1849 In the same act of Congress that made Minnesota a Territory, the Minnesota State Law Library was founded. The library is the oldest continuing library in the state and one of Minnesota's oldest institutions.

1853 Minnesota's first prison, the Minnesota Territorial Prison, opened in Stillwater and operated until 1914, when it was replaced with a new prison in Bayport. Today there are seven prisons for adult males (Faribault, Lino Lakes, Oak Park Heights, St. Cloud, Rush City, Stillwater and Willow River/Moose Lake. Willow River is the site of a boot camp for adult males and females). There is one adult female facility (Shakopee) and two juvenile male facilities (Red Wing and Togo).

1862 Thirty-eight Santee Sioux, found guilty of raping and murdering settlers, were hanged in Mankato on Dec. 26 in a mass execution witnessed by a large crowd of Minnesotans. It was the largest one-day execution in American history.

1876 The James-Younger gang attempted to rob the First National Bank of Northfield on Sept. 7. The gang escaped and split up. The Younger brothers were eventually captured and sentenced to 25 years in Stillwater prison.

1906 Capital punishment was last used in Minnesota. It was abolished in 1911, when life imprisonment replaced "death by hanging."

1917 Rochester's first policewoman was hired as a social welfare worker. The position was abolished by the mayor in 1932.

1920 On June 15 in Duluth, police arrested several black men accused of raping a white woman. That evening, three of them were taken from jail by a mob and lynched. The killings made headlines throughout the country. In 2003, the city of Duluth erected a memorial to the murdered men.

1929 The Minnesota State Patrol was created, and Earl Brown, sheriff of Hennepin County, was appointed chief of the Highway Patrol. Brown appointed eight officers and readied the barn on his farm in Brooklyn Center as a training facility.

1933 Brainerd had its first bank holdup Oct. 23 when five gunmen robbed the First National of approximately $32,000 and made a clean getaway. The gang was believed to include Baby Face Nelson and other gangsters.

1934 The Trucker's Strike in Minneapolis, also known as the Minneapolis Teamsters' Strike, got explosive in late-May at the city market, where strikers clashed with police in one of the most violent riots in state history. The battle lasted two days, leaving 200 injured and four dead. The strike marked a turning point in state and national labor history and legislation.

1952 The "Drunkometer," forerunner of today's Intoxilyzer, was first used by the Minneapolis Police Department.

122

About the Authors

Merle Minda

Merle Minda is a Twin Cities writer and marketing consultant. Formerly president of Minda Associates, her own public relations agency, she became a senior executive at Fleishman Hillard Public Relations, one of the three largest PR agencies in the world, when they acquired her company in 1998. Earlier, Merle was director of advertising and promotion for Minnesota Public Radio and executive director of the Metropolitan Arts Alliance. She led a national arts-as-rehabilitation program in correctional institutions and served as a national panelist and consultant for the National Endowment for the Arts, a director of the Playwrights' Center, Minneapolis, and advisor to the League of Women Voters. Merle has written about travel, food, décor, lifestyle, people and business for publications including *Twin Cities Business*, *Star Tribune*, *MARQ Magazine* and *Twin Cities Luxury & Fashion*.

Sheri O'Meara

Sheri O'Meara is editor of The Minnesota Series, and author or co-author of *Storms!*, *Storms 2* and *Media Tales*. She is also currently editor of *Minnesota Meetings and Events* magazine and has served as founding editor of monthly publications for K102-FM (where she was recognized by *Billboard* magazine for her work on *Minnesota Country* magazine), Sun Country Airlines and SimonDelivers. As editor of *Format Magazine*, she covered Minnesota's advertising and media industries for 10 years, the magazine receiving a Crystal Clarion Award from Minnesota Women in Communications. She has managed magazines for organizations including the Guthrie Theater and Minnesota Orchestra, and has written for a variety of Twin Cities publications. Sheri is also lead singer in the Twin Cities-based Celtic band Locklin Road.

More Crimes Coming ...

Watch for *Famous Crimes 2* coming up in the Minnesota Series. Including stories about:

• **The James-Younger gang's Northfield raid.** This botched robbery of the First National Bank of Northfield in 1876 eventually put an end to Jesse James and his gang, and landed the Younger brothers in Stillwater prison.

• **The case of Sarah Jane Olson ... aka Kathleen Soliah.** The former member of the Symbionese Liberation Army went underground and became a fugitive for 23 years. She built a life with her husband and daughters in St. Paul, an active member of the community, until her capture in 1999.

• **The murder of Barbara Lund.** One of Minnesota's most famous families was in the news in 1992 when Russell Lund Jr. was charged with the double homicide of his estranged wife and her boyfriend.

Plus, stories about:

• **The disappearance of Jacob Wetterling** (left)
• **The Eunice Kronholm kidnapping of 1970s**
• **The case of Dr. Douglas Simmons in Sunfish Lake**
• **The Jordan child abuse case**
• **The disappearance of television anchor Jodie Huisentruit, and more.**

Coming Up Next in The Minnesota Series:

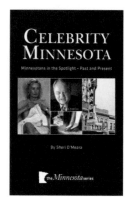

Don't miss our next book, *Celebrity Minnesota*, which chronicles the personalities and shows that made our state famous. Read about **Jessica Lange, Judy Garland, Peter Graves, F. Scott Fitzgerald, Tippi Hedren, John Madden, Tiny Tim** and more in this edition of The Minnesota Series.

Also watch for:

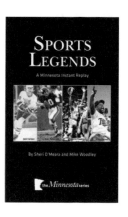

In *Sports Legends* read about the **Lakers, Vikings, Twins, Gophers, Duluth Eskimos**, the notorious **Fighting Saints** of the WHA, the **Fighting Pike** and everything in between. *Sports Legends* covers Minnesota sports and personalities from the legendary to the obscure in this edition of The Minnesota Series.

Political Stars

From famous families (the Mondales, Humphreys and Colemans) to the "Rudys" (Perpich and Boschwitz) to Minnesota's first congresswoman (Coya Knutson) to our most colorful governor ever (Jesse Ventura)—Minnesota politicians make for the most remarkable stories. **Don't miss these engaging tales as well as the inside stories of Eugene McCarthy, Paul Wellstone, Al Franken and others!**

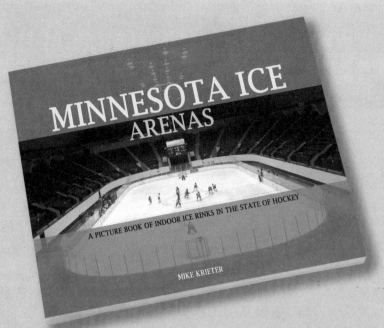